America in the Last days
The Jonah Nation

~ A Message of Hope ~

America In the Last Days: The Jonah Nation $21.95

Copyright ©2020 by Dr. Peter Wyns

To contact the author, please write to the below postal or email address:

Great Reward Publishing - *a ministry of Christians For Messiah Ministries*

PO Box 36324

Rock Hill, SC 29732

email: wynusa@comporium.net

All scriptures taken from the New International Version unless otherwise noted. Scriptures taken from the Holy Bible, New International Version ®.

All rights reserved. No part of this publication may be reproduced without prior permission of Great Reward Publishing or Dr. Peter Wyns.

First Great Reward Publishing edition published 2015.

Cover Design by: Rebecca Barrett

Editing by: Scott Dawson

Manufactured in the United States of America by IngramSpark.

ISBN: 978-0-9915421-2-3

Contents

Dedication		5
Introduction		7

Born With Purpose

Chapter One	Fanatical Muslims Attack Jonah	13
Chapter Two	Hidden Messages	21
Chapter Three	Jonah And America	28
Chapter Four	Two Of A Kind	35
Chapter Five	The Preacher	40
Chapter Six	The Dove	46
Chapter Seven	Nation Forming	52
Chapter Eight	Religious Persecution In Europe	57
Chapter Nine	The Purpose Of America	66
Chapter Ten	Exceptionalism In America	72
Chapter Eleven	Exceptional Freedom	83
Chapter Twelve	America - The Hero Nation	92
Chapter Thirteen	America's Missionaries	102
Chapter Fourteen	America's Support For Israel	108
Chapter Fifteen	Jonah Said No	125
Chapter Sixteen	Asleep At The Wheel	131

Running Away From God

Chapter Seventeen	America In The Bible	137
Chapter Eighteen	America And The Seven Churches	141

Chapter Nineteen	Disqualified Leaders	148
Chapter Twenty	Wake Up Jonah	155
Chapter Twenty-one	Can The White House Wake Up?	161

Judgment Over America

Chapter Twenty-two	Dark Clouds Coming	169
Chapter Twenty-three	What Have We Done?	174
Chapter Twenty-four	Two Kinds Of Judgment	183
Chapter Twenty-five	Jonah Overboard	191
Chapter Twenty-six	Ananias And Sapphira Sunday	198
Chapter Twenty-seven	America Overboard	205

Rescue And Revival

Chapter Twenty-eight	When All Hope Fails	215
Chapter Twenty-nine	The Beginning Of Birth Pains	220
Chapter Thirty	A Personal Revival	227
Chapter Thirty-one	The Jonah Revival	232
Chapter Thirty-two	Revival In Israel	238
Chapter Thirty-three	International Revival	248
Chapter Thirty-four	The Greatest Revival Ever	256
Chapter Thirty-five	America - A History Of Revival	264
Chapter Thirty-six	America's Coming Revival	271
Chapter Thirty-seven	America Makes The Millennium	278
Chapter Thirty-eight	America In The Millennium	285

End Notes   294 - 297

Dedication

I dedicate 'America in the Last Days', to my grandchildren. At this moment, Joy and I have thirteen.

It is said that God has no grandchildren, only children, and they are His children. Each one is a precious treasure to Him and to us. They have a powerful godly heritage and are being raised by outstanding parents. Each is growing in a creative atmosphere of faith and love. Even though, at the writing of this book, they are young, the grace of God rests upon them and, each, in their own way, has a unique relationship with Him.

Three of these children live in Canada, and the rest in the United States. The divide between these nations will not hinder the life-flow of end-time anointing and purpose that will shine through them. They will be part of the next great revival.

While these grandchildren have an amazing foundation, none of them are a copy of their parents or grandparents. Each is an original, created for purpose and trained for leadership. In their time they will minister with fresh anointing.

We are proud of them. Their names are Levi Wyns, Jacob Enns, Olivia Wyns, Judah Enns, Ethan Enns, Micah Enns, Merah Enns, Emma Wyns, Elisheva Wyns, Asher Enns, Hannah Wyns, Jonah Wyns, and Jameson Wyns.

All My Love,

"Papa" -   Dr. Peter Wyns

Introduction

America in the Last Days - The Jonah Nation

A Message of Hope

As this book is being written, international events are heating up. By the 30th of September 2015, the U.S. government solidified an agreement with Iran to postpone their nuclear enrichment program. This agreement was sharply criticized and resisted by the government of Israel who claimed the deal would only hurt Israel. They believe it provides a pathway that enabled Iran to have a nuclear bomb sometime in the future. Iran's goal is to destroy Israel. The deal was seen by many as a lack of support and protection for Israel; it only made Israel more vulnerable.

Since Israel became a nation in 1948, the USA has been her greatest ally. God connected the USA with Israel and whenever America fails her, judgment strikes the homeland. This has happened dozens of times and this incident proved to be no different.

A judgment came to America. At the same time that the Iran nuclear deal was ratified, Hurricane Joaquin flooded South Carolina with, what was called, "a thousand year flood." It was said to be the worst flood in South Carolina's history. Almost twenty people died and billions of dollars in property damages were left in Joaquin's wake.

There is no doubt that this is a prophetic time for Israel, America and the world at large. Every major political, geological and economic event we see is a product of cause and effect; we cannot escape it. For believers in the USA the question of the hour is, 'How will America act and react as the end-time purposes of God race forward to their forgone prophetic conclusion?'

That is what '<u>America in the Last Days</u>', is all about. Dr. Peter Wyns, the grandson of the late Derek Prince, takes us through the scriptures and the history of America to bring us a message of hope for America.

At a time when many Bible teachers are emphasizing gloom and doom for the USA, this book paints a brighter picture. To illustrate America's disposition, Dr. Wyns compares the future of the USA with the story of Jonah.

- Like Jonah, America has an amazing calling.
- Like Jonah, America is running away from God.
- Like Jonah, America is asleep in the proverbial bottom of the boat, or at the wheel.
- Like with Jonah, judgment will come to America.
- Like with Jonah, America will repent and be rescued by God.
- Like with Jonah, America will rise with amazing authority to preach the gospel and help lead the great end-time revivals.

Dr. Peter Wyns shows us in the Bible, God's promise of end-time revivals. He takes us through the exceptional history of America and points to God's laws of sowing and reaping.

It is easy to recognize America's failures, but God also sees her valiant exploits, and He does not forget.

It is time for the church to embrace a victorious eschatology. '<u>America in the Last Days</u>' will inspire faith and help posture you to be in step with heaven. It's time to embrace a message of hope for America.

Acknowledgments

I wish to acknowledge a few people who have worked with me as volunteers. These good friends have helped me get 'America In The Last Days' ready for print.

Rebecca Barrett has been such an amazing worker. She has helped me with many art projects. Rebecca worked diligently to put together the layout and design for the cover of this book. I am very grateful.

And to Scott Dawson, who read through the manuscript and edited it. He not only assisted me in the technical editing of the text, but also gave valuable feedback as to the subject matter and content. I know it was a labor of love. Thank you Scott.

And to Jesse Enns who is my son-in-law and coworker in the ministry. As always, he has been so helpful in the editing, formatting and with the theological content of this book.

And to those who have partnered with Joy and I in the ministry, by giving financially.

The generosity of many people enabled 'America in the Last Days' to be published. I am so grateful to all of you.

Thank you,

Dr. Peter Wyns

Part 1

Born With Purpose

Chapter 1

Fanatical Muslims Attack Jonah

Jonah's Tomb

All three religions - Judaism, Christianity and Islam - esteem Jonah as a prophet sent by God. Perhaps that is the reason why his tomb survived for thousands of years. It survived, the military invasions of dozens of armies, two horrifying world wars, earthquakes and extreme anti-Semitism that continued throughout Europe for dozens of centuries. So many anti-Semitic rulers ravaged Europe and the Middle East, destroying every semblance of Jewish heritage, especially synagogues and tombs.

I remember visiting a Jewish cemetery in Czechoslovakia in 1989. Every tombstone had been smashed, as if a crowd of violent men had spent days vandalizing it with sledge hammers. It was not that one stone, or a family group of stones was demolished; it was the entire cemetery. I could still make out the edges of Jewish Stars and Menorahs and fragments of Hebrew letters that seemed to cry out to me from the rubble.

Like almost everywhere in Europe and the Middle East, at some point, hatred for the Jews became volatile and their heritage was attacked, their tombs were desecrated. The tomb of Jonah, however, endured. His mausoleum, in the middle of a totalitarian Muslim nation, was left unscathed. Against all odds, it survived thousands of years, that is, until just this past year. On July 24, 2014, the so-called Islamic State, (ISIS) terrorists, a group of Islamic extremists, vandalized and destroyed the 2700-year-old tomb of Jonah the prophet. The tomb was, all but hidden, in a Muslim mosque, in the city of Mosul, Iraq; the city that once was called Nineveh. The modern outside world knew little of it. To my knowledge, no Christian pastor or Jewish rabbi, that I knew, even realized its existence. On that day, however, the tomb became a target. It was first attacked with sledgehammers and then explosives.

Christianity flourished in the region, as early as the second century and by the sixth century Mosel became the Episcopal seat of the Nestorian-Christian faith. Originally, the building site that venerated the tomb of Jonah was a church. When the Muslims conquered the land in the seventh century, they turned it into a mosque, but continued to honor the memory of the great prophet. This was arguably, the resting place of the greatest preacher of all time.

The Devil is Furious

It is no accident, that having survived more than two and a half millennium, Jonah's memorial was destroyed this year. The devil is focused and furious because of what this man Jonah accomplished and more to the point, what is about to happen in connection with the on-going spirit and calling of Jonah. The dragon is afraid; the time has come, Heaven is focused on his ruin and he knows it. He is furious.

The spiritual conflict on the planet has become more intense and a generation of new Jonahs is about to emerge. They will be revival-starters, mercy-extenders, powerhouse prophets, and anointed preachers. I am convinced that a great number of them will come from the United States of America.

Scripture tells us of a future time when the devil becomes enraged. It happens when he realizes that his defeat is just around the corner. We read of his reactionary fury in the book of Revelation. It says, **"Then the dragon was enraged at the woman and went off to make war against the rest of her offspring - those who obey God's commandments and hold to the testimony of Jesus. And the dragon stood on the shore of the sea."** Rev. 12:17

The prophecy tells of a future date when Satan is cast down from the heavens. He is furious and he lashes out. From time to time, the devil understands what is about to happen, and in reaction, he attacks the people of God in order to hinder the ministry, that inevitably, is aimed against him. We are now living in such a time. That is why the tomb of Jonah was destroyed and why believers are being slaughtered in various countries around the world.

The tomb has been destroyed and it was not an accident. What does the devil know that most Christians do not know? I will tell you; Jonah's army is coming, and it will signal the beginning of the end for him.

The Story of Jonah

Some Christians think that the story of Jonah and the great fish is the stuff of fables and folklore, but Jesus Himself validated the truth of the story. He said, **"As Jonah was three days and three nights in the belly of a huge fish, so the Son of Man will be three days and three nights in the heart of the earth. The men of Nineveh will stand up at the judgment with this generation and condemn it; for they repented at the preaching of Jonah, and now one greater than Jonah is here."** Mt. 12:40-42.

If we believe that Jesus died and was in the earth for three days, then we must also believe that Jonah was in the huge fish for three days. Jesus confirmed both events in the same teaching.

As we look back, we discover the man of God, the prophet Jonah. He was the son of a Jew named Amittai and was born in Gath Hepher, not far from the towns of Nazareth and Cana of Galilee. Gath Hepher is situated alongside the great end-time, war-valley, the Jezreel, the valley of Armageddon. He was from the tribe of Zebulon. Jonah was an actual man; we know his lineage, we know where he was born, and we know what he did.

The Jewish Blessing

Jonah was born into the nation that God chose to bless. The Israelites are God's chosen; they are blessed because of the patriarchs, and their gifts and calling cannot be revoked. Romans says, "**As far as election is concerned, they** [the Jewish people] **are loved on account of the patriarchs, for God's gifts and his call are irrevocable." Rom. 11:28**

Called to a Calling

People of faith understand the term; a calling from God is a special, predetermined intention for an individual or a people. It means that someone will be able to do something that is great; something that is extraordinary, and it will be unique to them.

It is when God literally calls you, or assigns you to a task, a mission, or a responsibility. Somehow, you hear His voice, and you know what you have to do. It becomes a great passion in your life. It may come in your youth or later in life, and it may come to you in a moment of time, or grow within you over time. It is an amazing privilege to be called by God, but the truth is, that every human is called in some measure, to do great things for God. Discovering and fulfilling your calling is one of the greatest and most fulfilling adventures in life.

The Jews are so blessed; they are called; they are endowed by their Creator. Their leadership is remarkable. I am always amazed to discover, for good or for bad, how so many Jews have left an astonishing mark on the world. Many have done evil things with the knowledge they had, but I prefer to focus on the good they have done. Permit me to focus on the subject of Nobel prizes. Although the number of Jews on the planet is minuscule compared to most other ethnic groups, they have, nevertheless, been awarded more Nobel prizes than any other ethnic group in the world. Twenty-two percent of all Nobel prizes have been awarded to Jews. They are definitely blessed by God.

When God Singles Out a Jew

As an ethnic group, the Jews are God's chosen people, but when God chooses one of them to do something special, that person becomes quite extraordinary. Jonah was a Jew with an extraordinary call of God on his life. That being said, the call of God is not always a sweet ride. The late Derek Prince, my grandfather used to say, "There are two things that God will call us to that are always inconvenient; one is judgment day, and the other is the call to ministry."

Both Jonah and the USA have a special calling and purpose, and it seems that both, were and are inconvenient. When anyone is called by God, they will have to deal with many emotional rollercoaster rides, and lots of rejection.

Prophets Suffer Rejection

Of all of the ministries God may call us to, the call of the prophet is the one that generally, experiences the most rejection. Prophets of the Lord must be bold and courageous. They must proclaim the word of the Lord whether it will be accepted or not. As if to make it even more challenging, they might be given a word that will be uncomfortable and even adversarial for the one for whom it is intended. No one likes to make enemies and no one likes to be judged, but every time a prophet speaks he or she is judged. The Bible even tells us to judge the words of the prophet. **"Let two or three prophets speak and let the others judge." 1 Cor. 14:29**

This means the life of a genuine prophet may be a lonely one. People may hold their friendship at a distance. A Jewish prophet faces double rejection, first because he is a prophet, and second, because he is a Jew. Jews have often been rejected by people of other nations. If not right away, anti-Semitism may rise up over time. Perhaps other people become jealous of the Jewish blessing. Perhaps they feel looked down on because they are not God's chosen people. Perhaps the success of their Jewish neighbors outshines them, or puts them in an inferior situation. Whatever the reason for the growing hatred toward the Jews, the dynamic is very real. Anti-Semitism has continued around the world and throughout history, and unfortunately, it is very much alive today.

Jonah was a prophet of the Lord and he was a Jewish prophet, so he faced double rejection. For Jonah, the problem was exacerbated even more because God commanded him to aim his prophetic gift in the direction of his national enemy. Nineveh was the capital city of the Syrians, the enemies of Israel. The Ninevites hated Jonah and would just as soon, kill him on sight, because he was a Jew. Even before they heard who he was, or what his message might be, they already despised him, simply because of his nationality. How in the world could Jonah be expected to go and prophesy judgment to those who might want to kill him? We will give more details concerning Jonah's dilemma, in another chapter.

All of these ingredients make a recipe for rejection, and Jonah had a cup full of it. He could not stand it and he ran from God. He ran from the pressure.

Rejecting the USA

The United States of America often deals with a similar dynamic. To start with, the success and blessings of God over the USA and her people are undeniable. She often champions good causes around the world, but is not always appreciated for it. Perhaps it is because, like the Jews, America has taken the lead economically, militarily and she influences dramatic changes in culture around the world, more than any other nation.

Whether seen as good or bad, the USA is extraordinary and others are jealous; some are even fearful of her. Many are incensed with anger and hatred toward America because of her strength and her intrusion into their personal and national affairs. Some religious and ethnic groups have come to hate America because they have such opposing ideologies. For example, not all rulers embrace democracy, individual freedom, the Christian community, or a capitalistic based economy. When the USA promotes these ideals she is often seen as an arrogant meddler in other people's business.

Like with Jonah, many in America have a sense of mission from God. They are compelled by faith or conscience to rescue the downtrodden and promote God-given values among the nations. That, however, is often construed as interference, and America is negatively labeled, 'the policemen of the world'. This is meant to be a derogatory term, however, policeman serving as they should, are only a blessing. in countries like present-day Libya, the level of crime, corruption, abuse and oppression is terrifying. It is because they have no adequate police force or government to protect them. The poor folk of that nation cry out for police protection but they receive none. They wish the USA would come and rescue them and help set their nation right. While many in the world wish they had what

the Americans can deliver, they still disdain them, and even wish for their destruction.

Jonah and America have much in common. It is not only reflected in their early disposition, but also in their future destiny and calling. We will look into the life of Jonah and discover a pattern that is yet to be played-out in the United States. Both reveal a story of waywardness and rebellion, but in the end, Jonah and America straighten out with amazing resolve. Both experience their God-intended mission.

Chapter 2

Hidden Messages

Obvious and Hidden Messages

America is not mentioned in the Bible, neither are computers or cars, yet the future is mentioned. The world we live in is alluded to in the scriptures. The future is there, although sometimes hidden.

Some prophecies have an obvious meaning like Daniel's prophecy about the end of time. He writes, **"Multitudes who sleep in the dust of the earth will awake; some to everlasting life, others to shame and everlasting contempt. Those who are wise will shine like the brightness of the heavens, and those who lead many to righteousness, like the stars forever and ever ... Many will go here and there to increase knowledge."** Da. 12:4

These verses reveal four obvious things about the future.

1. They tell us there will be a resurrection of the dead.

2. Some will be resurrected to life and some to everlasting shame.

3. These scriptures tell of an end-time revival, because believers will lead many to righteousness.

4. These verses point to a dramatic increase in travel and a massive increase of information. Travel and information have increased with explosive proportions just as God's word predicted.

Not So Obvious Messages

Like the above-mentioned verses, there are obvious prophetic messages in the Bible. Then, there are messages in the Bible that are not so obvious. The Apostle Peter received a prophetic vision, but its meaning was hidden. Let us review Peter's story.

At a time when Peter was hungry, God gave him a vision of unclean animals and told him to get up and eat them. In the vision, the animals were lowered before him on a sheet. The Bible says, **"Then a voice told him, 'Get up Peter, kill and eat.'" Acts 10:13**

Three times the sheet was lowered with animals on it and three times Peter was told to kill and eat them. To Peter, this was an unreasonable command. It was unheard of, and extremely difficult because Peter was a Law observant, kosher -keeping Jew, and these were unclean animals. He was forbidden to eat these unclean animals. **"'Surely not Lord!' Peter replied, 'I have never eaten anything impure or unclean.' The voice spoke to him a second time, 'Do not call anything impure that God has called clean.' This happened three times." Acts 10:14-16**

There was a hidden meaning in the vision and it became clear over time. It was not about eating food at all, but about receiving non-Jewish people. While Peter was wondering about the vision, a few non-Jewish men began calling him from outside the house. Peter met them and ended up going with them to the port city of Caesarea. There, he met Cornelius, the Roman centurion, and told him and his family about Jesus Christ.

In time, Peter realized that the vision was not what it seemed. It was about Gentiles coming to Christ and not about unclean food items. God was preparing Peter for a shift in his thinking. Before that time, only Jews were being received into the church. Now, God was extending the gospel to all nations and to all peoples. The message of Peter's vision was like a riddle that needed to be solved. So while Daniel's prophecy about the future was obvious, Peter's required further revelation.

The Powerful Number Three

There are details about Peter's story that are even more hidden and only a studious disciple would catch them. For example, the sheet of unclean animals that was lowered and the words spoken to Peter to kill and eat, was given three times. If God gives a message three times, it is extremely serious; it is something that God is emphasizing.

This is seen throughout the Scriptures; every word should be established by the mouth of two or three witnesses. Let us look at the number three. For example, Jesus prayed three times in the Garden of Gethsemane, Paul prayed three times for the removal of the thorn in his flesh, and Esther called the Jews to fast and pray for three days. Praying fervently about something three times, means you have prayed as you should. The prayer request has been properly brought before the Lord and now you should back away and leave it with Him, unless He says otherwise.

The prayer example is only the beginning; Jesus' ministry lasted three years, His cross was one of three, and 'King of the Jews,' was written above his cross in three languages. His body was three days in the tomb and Jonah was three days in the belly of the great fish .

God comes to us in three persons, His authority has three spheres. He is omnipresent (all present), omniscient (all knowing) and omnipotent (all powerful.) All matter that God created has three dimensions, (height, width, and depth), and time itself is past, present and future. These are God established truths and they are final.

If you have the same dream three times, you had better pay close attention to it, it is surely a serious message from God. The number three is used by God to fully establish a truth about something. Good or bad, it becomes an established communication, a definitive demonstration, an emphasized focus or a totally settled issue. God has made the number three powerful!

Peter saw the sheet with unclean animals three times, and he knew the message was extremely important. Forgive me, but I continue to belabor the point regarding the number three, to prove that there are hidden messages in the Bible.

The children of Israel took three-day journeys, as they travelled through the wilderness after leaving Egypt. Later they were required, every year, to go up to Jerusalem for three pilgrim feasts. At this time in history, the Israelites, as a nation, have entered and reentered the Promised Land, three times. You will see, they are now established in the land - never to be removed from it again.

Before the rooster crowed, Jesus told Peter he would deny Him three times, and Peter was one of Jesus' three closest friends. David fought a lion, a bear, and a giant, before becoming king. Elijah, in the cave, faced a hurricane, an earthquake, and a forest fire, before he heard the still small voice of God. There are three possible types of temptation, the lust of the flesh, the lust of the eyes, and the boastful pride of life. All and every temptation is included in this list of three. The list that points to the importance of the number three goes on and on.

There is much to be said for Peter's sheet of unclean animals being lowered before him three times. Peter instinctively knew this vision was important because it happened three times. The message from God was confirmed and established but Peter had to figure it out and obey it. He dare not ignore what God was showing him. The process of discovery would fortify the fact that from now on, God was reaching out to the whole world and not just to Jews.

At first Peter received the vision at face value; he thought it was about unclean food. It came three times so the message went deep into his spirit. Then the Gentile men called to him from the gate. Peter knew what God was saying. It was a hidden message, but he got it. With confidence, he immediately went to Caesarea to bring the gift of God's Holy Spirit to those of a different race.

God often speaks to His people in riddles. He calls us to seek Him, hear his voice, and to enter into a dynamic personal relationship with him.

The Bible is Full of Hidden Messages

Millions of disciples are constantly reading the Bible to find the deeper meanings that are hidden in the text. Those meanings are treasures put there by God, and they belong to those who diligently search for deeper truth. These treasures, must not contradict the rest of the Bible, for God does not contradict Himself. If we receive a new revelation we must confirm that it fits the teachings of the rest of the Bible. That is a safeguard that keeps us from changing the meaning of scripture and creating false doctrines.

When these deeper truths are discovered they bring direction and strength to the disciple who finds them. Often prophetic words about the future are discovered through such a search, and because of it, God's people become more in-tune with Him and His purpose.

The story of Jonah and its similarities with America is such a find. The more you discover their commonality, the more God will reveal their future prophetic significance. Then you will know how to pray and partner with God for America in the last days.

Two Applications of the Bible

Allow me to explain this a little further. Every verse in the Bible has two applications; first, the application that fits its original purpose or intent. That is a message given, or a historical account in context for the time, culture, and for whom it was sent.

The second application for every verse in the Bible applies to anyone, anywhere at any given time. The second application can fit any culture and any person. It must be received as the Holy Spirit makes it relevant and not as a tool to justify every personal action.

The word of God is not bound, and the Holy Spirit speaking to us from the scriptures is one of the ways that God communicates to His children. If you are a disciple of Christ, you have, no doubt, read a portion of scripture that God personalized just for you. It happens to millions of people every day.

Jonah and America

Through my studies, the Holy Spirit revealed that the story of America is like the story of Jonah. Like Jonah, America's greatness is often missed. I think the huge fish in the story of Jonah is admired by the world more than Jonah is. What he ended up doing is overlooked.

The USA is an extraordinary nation, and it will become even more so. Many only see her failures. They are focused more on her shortcomings than her amazing accomplishments. Some, on the other hand, focus on the judgments of God that are approaching, and fail to see America's end-time redemptive purpose.

Like Jonah, God chose America with greatness in mind. Like Jonah, the USA is poised for God's sovereign purpose, and like Jonah, America will fulfill her calling at the appointed time.

Like the hidden message in the story of Peter's vision, there are hidden messages in the story of Jonah. These messages will give the church in America fresh insight and direction. I invite you to look at Jonah and discover the hidden future of America.

Chapter 3

Jonah And America

The Great Jonah

The book of Jonah has only forty-eight verses and eight of those are prayers and proclamations. Only forty verses are left to tell Jonah's story. His narrative, however, is known the world over; everyone knows of Jonah and the whale. Unfortunately, people focus little on the rest of Jonah's story; they do not know his legacy. The truth is that few men have been more powerful than he.

When we think of who in history, over one weekend, was instrumental in cleaning up the lives of such a huge multitude of people, we discover that Jonah has no rivals. Jonah's coming to Nineveh resulted in an explosive revival that in scope and size, to date, has no equal.

The Jonah Syndrome

So the story unfolds. The children are snuggled and gathered and the storyteller begins his account of the ancient tale. A hush settles like a heavy fog upon the little ones and even the adults in the corners of the room are captivated. They are mesmerized by the image of the great fish suddenly appearing from behind a wall of torrential rain. He is coming out of the storm with one purpose. He has an assignment. He has come to swallow the man who is running away from God.

The violence of the storm is overpowering and the sailors fear for their lives. They have thrown their entire cargo and all of their possessions overboard, but it has not helped. They are asking who has brought them such devastating, bad luck. When they find out that it is Jonah, they wonder what he could have done to bring such wrath upon them.

From this horrific scene of ill fortune, echoes the ghostly name, Jonah. From now on and forever, Jonah has been immortalized, as the human symbol of bad luck. Every person from here on out who is seen as a root cause of failure, is likely to be called a Jonah. This is called the Jonah Syndrome. Superstitions are powerful and this superstition says that when a, so called, Jonah is on your team, you don't stand a chance, you always have trouble, you are destined for failure and despair.

The misconception about Jonah bringing bad luck is so pervasive that the rest of the story seems to drop off into the mire of insignificance. Most people miss the important details, they simply overlook the outcome of the narrative.

The United States is Similar

The United States has a similar disposition; like Jonah, she is incredibly unique. Her exceptionalism is amazing, yet it is largely overlooked because of her failures.

Jealousies and opposing ideologies have also conspired to draw attention away from America's greatness. On top of this, there are many attempts to rewrite the history of America. They call it revisionism and, in this case, it is designed to change the historical facts regarding America's biblical beginnings and godly foundations. Some who oppose a Judeo-Christian lifestyle want all acknowledgements to Christianity and God removed from the national consciousness of America. There is a concerted effort to keep the God-centered legacy of the USA from future generations. Many do not want Americans celebrating her greatness and they certainly do not want Americans to be emboldened to accomplish even more great things in the name of Christ.

Jonah Can Help Us

Jonah can help us. By studying his life we discover a common thread between Jonah, the man and America, the nation. Both have been called and sent by God. Both are destined to accomplish great and wondrous things.

The prophet, Jonah was sent to the sinful city of Nineveh and, I believe, America has four amazing mission task that involve other nations.

1. America has been sent to help feed and clothe the poor of the world.

2. She has been commissioned to help protect the weaker nations and to promote liberty and freedom for all.

3. She has been called to stand with and to bless Israel.

4. The USA is called to spread the good news of the Gospel of the kingdom of God to all who will receive.

Jonah's Story is America's Story

The story of Jonah can be illustrated by five distinct experiences. These same experiences will become the narrative of the Unites States. God's dealings with Jonah and America are inseparable.

1. Jonah and the U.S. had and have, an incredible calling from God.

2. Jonah ran from God and from his God-given purpose. Today, the USA is running away from God and is running from her purpose and destiny.

3. Jonah was judged. He was thrown overboard and swallowed by a great fish. The United States will be judged to the extent that all hope for life and safety will fade away.

4. Jonah repented and prayed from the belly of the great fish. He was forgiven and restored to life again. Likewise, America will repent. There will be a rebirth and a resurrection in America and it will begin with the church.

5. Jonah went forward and became the greatest preacher of all time. The day will come when thousands of anointed Jonah-like preachers will rise up across the USA. They will preach like Jonah and witness unprecedented revival among the nations. The following is a glimpse of America's calling.

America's Poem

It seems to be forgotten, the poem that I like to call America's poem. Has it been ignored and swept under the carpet, because trying to fulfill the mandate of the poem is too much trouble, and way too expensive? Perhaps it is no longer politically correct, but this poem still reflects the calling and destiny of America. The USA is called to be a God-loving, God-fearing, and God-partnering nation. The poem I speak of, is (in my opinion) the insufficiently titled poem, 'The New Colossus', by Emma Lazarus written in 1883. I believe these words sound forth the intentions of God for America. The poem was written to animate the Statue of Liberty, who

Emma Lazarus calls, the 'Mother of Exiles'. The Statue is America. She is welcoming the forsaken refugees of the world, and she stands in stark contrast to the ancient pompous, Greek bronze statue, "The Colossus".

The New Colossus

Not like the brazen giant of Greek fame,

With conquering limbs astride from land to land;

Here at our sea-washed, sunset gates shall stand

A mighty woman with a torch, whose flame

Is the imprisoned lightning, and her name

Mother of Exiles. From her beacon-hand

Glows world-wide welcome; her mild eyes command

The air-bridged harbor that twin cities frame.

"Keep, ancient lands, your storied pomp!"

cries she

With silent lips. "Give me your tired, your poor,

Your huddled masses yearning to breathe free,

The wretched refuse of your teeming shore.

Send these, the homeless, tempest-tossed to me,

I lift my lamp beside the golden door!"

Emma Lazarus, 1883

Who Was She?

As detailed on her Wikipedia page,[i] Emma Lazarus was born on July 22, 1849. She was the fourth of seven children of Moses Lazarus and Esther Nathan, Sephardic Jews whose families, originally from Portugal, had been settled in New York since the colonial period. Besides writing notable poems, Lazarus wrote novels and two five-act plays including *The Dance to Death*, a dramatization of a German short story about burning Jews in Nordhausen during the Black Death.

Lazarus began to be more interested in her Jewish ancestry after reading the George Eliot novel *Daniel Deronda,* and as she heard of the Russian pogroms that followed the assassination of Tsar Alexander II in 1881. As a result of this anti-Semitic violence, thousands of destitute Ashkenazi Jews emigrated from the Russian Pale of Settlement to New York, leading Lazarus to write articles on the subject as well as the book, *Songs of the Semite* (1882). Lazarus began at this point to advocate on behalf of indigent Jewish refugees and helped establish the Hebrew Technical Institute in New York to provide vocational training to help destitute Jewish immigrants become self-supporting.

She is best known for "The New Colossus". Its lines appear on a bronze plaque in the pedestal of the Statue of Liberty, placed in 1903. Lazarus' close friend Rose Hawthorne Lathrop was inspired by "The New Colossus" to found the Dominican Sisters of Hawthorne.

Rose Hawthorne founded the ministry designated to helping patients with terminal cancer. To this day the Sisters of Hawthorne refuse government funding or social welfare for their work.

Emma Lazarus was a powerful forerunner of the Zionist movement. She argued for the creation of a Jewish homeland thirteen years before Theodor Herzl began to use the term Zionism.

Lazarus died on November 19, 1887 at the age of 38, after a prolonged illness, most likely from Hodgkin's Lymphoma.

Echoes of the Past, Prophecy for the Future

Emma Lazarus echoed the national conscience of caring for the poor that was given to America by God. The Lord has commissioned the USA to help the needy, the oppressed and the downtrodden of the world, and to a great measure, she has done it.

Emma Lazarus' words reflect the heart of God but also echo the passion and desire of many Americans. More than a few have lost their way and are running from destiny but the spirit behind the words of the poem will be championed once again. Following her national adjustment, America will rise like Jonah and be used of God like no other. If you are a praying person, pray to that end.

Chapter 4
Two Of A Kind

Jesus' Death and Jonah's Fish

God has eternally connected the death of his Son and the swallowing of Jonah by the mega-fish. Once awakened to this revelation, the connection cannot be overlooked. Both stories are so monumental that they have become international in scope and have been passed on from generation to generation. The suffering of Jonah points to Christ, and the passion of Christ is referenced back to Jonah. Let's investigate this sovereign connection.

Jesus Only

For humanity, the greatest act in history is the sacrifice of a lamb. Jesus, the Lamb of God is the Creator's special gift to the world. Because of this sacrifice, humanity is redeemed, or brought back to the blessings of God. **"For God so loved the world that He gave His only begotten Son". Jn. 3:16**

"It was not with perishable things such as silver or gold that you were redeemed from the empty way of life handed down to you from your forefathers, but with the precious blood of Christ, a lamb without blemish or defect. He was chosen before the creation of the world, but was revealed in these last times for your sake." 1 Pe. 1:18-20

The act of Christ's redemptive death was not a repair, an after-thought, or an adjustment to counter balance the unexpected failures of humanity. God, in eternity past, designed a perfect plan that would yield the greatest benefits. Christ's death was the absolute solution and the only cure for the sins of the world. Only through faith, and only through Jesus Christ, can a person come to God. Jesus is the way to the Father and to eternal life and there simply is no other way. Speaking of Jesus, scripture says, **"Salvation is found in no one else, for there is no other name under heaven given to men by which we must be saved." Acts 4:12**

Only one path leads to life, and that is how the future kingdom of God will be populated. No other path, no other name, and no other sacrifice, will bring a person to paradise. Ultimately, everyone who makes it there will be justified, sanctified, and glorified. They will become like Jesus; they will have Jesus' DNA.

I am sure that many people throughout history have tried to help God out by coming up with a better idea. Some may feel that God's plan is not the best one possible. Many struggle with the idea of total surrender to the Christian God. They may even feel that God is unjust to design only one plan and expect everyone in the world to acclimate to it.

The truth is that no better plan is possible. God is determined to have a future kingdom where all of its inhabitants will shine with righteousness, peace and joy. He insists that those who are part of His kingdom are there because they want to be there, and not because they are forced. He has no intention of robbing a person of their free will to choose.

The plan is so perfect. You see, everyone can try to be perfect on their own, but they will come to the realization that it is impossible. Then they are invited to choose Jesus and to enter God's pathway to perfection. All who follow this path are not just forgiven of their sins and remade in the image of Christ, they also become joint heirs with Christ of everything that is great and wonderful.

If you have not yet surrendered your will to Christ, then you might not like your options, but this is God's plan. It is for all humanity and it is perfect. **"He is patient with you, not wanting anyone to perish, but everyone to come to repentance." 2 Pe. 3:9**

Every aspect of this plan is made available through the death of Christ on the cross. That is why the greatest act in history is the sacrifice of a lamb. The Bible says it like this. **"He who did not spare his own Son, but gave him up for us all-how will he not also, along with him, graciously give us all things." Rom. 8:32**

Jesus Chose Jonah

Of course Jesus knew of His coming death and of all it would yield for the human race, when he talked about Jonah to the crowds. He could have compared his death on the cross to the story of Noah, Abraham, or Moses, but the sign He gave the world, and the one He personally identified with, was that Jonah. He said: "[No sign] **will be given... except the sign of the prophet Jonah. For as Jonah was three days and three nights in the belly of a huge fish, so the Son of Man will be three days and three nights in the heart of the earth. The men of Nineveh will stand up in judgment with this generation and condemn it; for they repented at the preaching of Jonah, and now one greater than Jonah is here." Mt. 12:39-41**

As we contemplate Christ's sacrifice as the greatest act in history, and that it was planned before the foundations of the world, we receive new insight regarding the scriptures. We realize that from the first family, through the journeys of the Jews, to the proclamations of the prophets, Christ's death was foretold. In fact, everything in the Bible points, in some way, to the cross and all scripture was planned and given to us for that purpose.

The story of Jonah, before it happened, was designed to prefigure Christ's death on the cross. Jonah was chosen, not just by Jesus as an afterthought, but by God in eternity past. He was the chosen one whose story would become the sign that would point to the death, burial, and resurrection of Christ Jesus. He was special, like no one else.

Gath Hepher

The birthplace of Jonah was Gath Hepher. It is now an archeological site five miles northeast of Nazareth and just a mile from Cana of Galilee. It is situated on the borders of Zebulon, and like so many other small villages of ancient Israel, it is seemingly insignificant. It was, however, not insignificant to God. Gath Hepher was the, all but hidden, yet famous birthplace of the great prophet.

Cradled in the ancient hills of Galilee, archeologists have discovered the ruins of two synagogues near the Gath Hepher site. Although synagogues had not yet been instituted in the time of Jonah, their later installation in the region verifies the spiritual legacy of the place. They point to the likelihood that Jonah had religious training and was no doubt chosen by a rabbi to be his dedicated student, his disciple.

Everyone of great calling needs a strong foundation but, like with so many students, Jonah had a direct link with God, and would soon surpass the spiritual scope of his teacher. Jonah was intellectual, outspoken, and no doubt the greatest of his rabbi's theological debaters.

He had a gift, he heard from God and he was very courageous, almost to the point of defiance. Some, in the community did not like him, but could not take a strong stand against him for he was brilliant and godly. That is the early life of any true prophet, and before Jonah received the word to go to Nineveh, he was already known as Jonah, the prophet from Gath Hepher.

Unknown Greatness

Usually, we underestimate the far-reaching greatness of the children and youth around us. Unfortunately, many, if not most become distracted and never reach their full purpose in life. Sometimes, God refuses to let an individual wander off, perhaps because they have a purpose beyond their personal benefit, and God sees to it that His plan is enacted. Some individuals have been chosen to be part of God's bigger plan so they will not find it easy to sidestep Him.

Jonah was such a man. His spiritual gifts as a speaker and as a prophet were so pronounced because God was grooming him for Nineveh and, even more so, to be an historical type of Christ. While other boys his age were focused on gathering in the olive harvest, or learning how to train a yoke of oxen, Jonah was dedicated to the purposes of God for Israel and for humanity. As a young man, he stood out as extraordinary, He was a man set aside for the purposes of God. Little did he know at the time that his name would go down in infamy.

Chapter 5

The Preacher

Chosen to Preach

When I was still a very young man, I was called by God into the ministry. At first, I was not chosen to be an apostle, a teacher, or even a pastor, I was called to be a preacher. In like manner, Paul, speaking of himself wrote, " **I am ordained a preacher" 1 Tim. 2:7 KJV**

 I was just fourteen, and had given my life to Christ less than a week before when God called me into the ministry. I was reading Rev. David Wilkerson's book, <u>The Cross and the Switchblade</u>, when God spoke to me. I had surrendered my life to God and knew that my life was no longer my own, so I was asking God what He wanted me to do and what He wanted me to be.

As part of my seeking God, I was fasting from food, and praying for direction. I had come home from school and had gone up to my bedroom, away from the dining table where the rest of the family would be eating supper.

That night, at eight o'clock, under the lights, I would be playing baseball. I was captain of the team, and my position was shortstop. I had my glove and ball in hand, so it is easy to understand why my mind drifted to the game, and I was not paying much attention to the book I was reading.

At first, I found the book boring, perhaps because I was so distracted. I was praying, fasting, seeking God, reading and thinking about baseball when suddenly, there on page eleven, the book came alive. I read that David Wilkerson was in New York, destined to help the gang related youth of the city. Suddenly, as the book read, Wilkerson stepped out onto a baseball field. The Holy Spirit began zoning in on me and I was immediately catapulted into a God moment.

I read with focused attention. David Wilkerson walked onto a baseball field and said. "On this baseball field, I will build my church." Then he looked out to center field, and said, " And my pulpit will be at shortstop."

I know, it may not mean much to some, but the Holy Spirit came upon me, I fell to my knees and rededicated my life to God as a preacher of the Gospel. I was called to stand behind a pulpit. That was my first ministry calling, and to this day, almost 45 years later, while I have doubted many things, I have never doubted my call to be a preacher.

Preachers

I feel an affinity with Jonah. I do not know about his full calling, but I am sure, excluding the baseball details, that Jonah's calling must have been like mine, only more so. I have, for the most part, found preaching to be a thrill and a creative passion that brings me great pleasure. It is my life, my calling, and my privilege. Although in the early days, I spent dozens of hours preparing sermons, there have been times when the word of God came to me with such ease. I have often been amazed at the profound effect that preaching God's word has had on others.

I have wondered why some preachers seem to be, in my opinion, so terrible at preaching. Some seem unable to preach their way out of a wet paper bag, and I must confess, that I have suffered a huge amount of boredom, as circumstances have forced me to sit and listened to many inadequate preachers along the way. I do feel for the larger body of Christ when I witness this.

In amazing contrast, I have been glued to my seat and totally captivated by some who have preached God's word so skillfully that I felt I was hearing straight from the Lord Himself. At times the room has been impregnated with the glory of God and I felt that the speaker should have preached for a much longer time. Those, moments seem to be less common in recent years. I have not witnessed too many great preachers in the last fifteen years. My unwavering faith on this subject, however, compels me to announce that the ministry of the great preacher will one day reemerge. When that day comes, it will be like a waterfall of powerful anointing and be like nothing ever experienced before. Oh, how I long for that day!

Sitting With Jonah

It must have been such a treat to sit and hear the prophet Jonah preach. No one living during his lifetime was more inspiring than he. Perhaps, only Jesus Himself could preach with such a silver tongue or such a depth of power.

Grandpa Derek Prince said that nothing was taught until something had been learned. He said that the gift of powerful teaching meant that profound revelation would be given with amazing simplicity. He always tried to communicate as if he was speaking to a fourteen year old. I have tried to emulate him. I wish I could have heard Jonah preach.

The real test of a preacher is in the end product. How many are converted, changed, inspired or powerfully motivated after they have heard the preacher? The ultimate purpose of every God-anointed sermon is change.

Without bringing change to the listener, the sermon must either be weak or it fell upon deaf ears. God's word does not return unto Him void, so if it came from God it will somehow produce change. The Bible instructs the preacher to speak, not with the words of man's wisdom, but as the Oracle of God. Under the anointing of the Holy Spirit, Peter said, **"If anyone speaks, let him speak as the oracles of God." 1 Pe. 4:11**

Jonah spoke like that. First, he was a well-established prophet and a prophet of Old Testament days was to be stoned to death if found to be lying. Jonah was received as a prophet by his countrymen, so we know he spoke the words of God. Secondly, he was a Bible preacher, one who spoke the oracles of God. His gift was likely underestimated by family and friends, and even by himself. I would have really enjoyed hearing him preach.

Preacher or Teacher

I think, as a side note, I should give my thoughts regarding the main difference between preaching and teaching. First of all, permit me to dispel a myth. Preaching is not more demonstrative than teaching, and teaching is not more academic or more organized than preaching. The full array of human personality may be incorporated in both the preacher and the teacher, and depending on the personality and training, one might be more gregarious and/or more academic or intellectual.

A study of the use of the word preacher and teacher in the Bible gives us a very different perspective. Here is an over simplification, but it will help us get a better perspective on the difference between the preacher and the teacher. I suggest that preaching is teaching the unsaved, and teaching is preaching to the saved. It is not the emotion, the volume, or the intellectual prowess that determines the difference between preacher and teacher, but rather to whom the message is given.

Jonah the Preacher

Hard work, study, in-depth meditation, intense prayer, and a dedicated focus on dynamic delivery, is essential for a preacher of the Gospel. Jonah had it all; he had been chosen, equipped and empowered by God with great gifting. My dad used to sit under the preaching of Smith Wigglesworth. He told me that Smith used to say to his disciples, "Preach like you are driving a nail into someone's forehead. Do not stop until you see the print of the hammer in their skin." Perhaps it was stated a bit over-dramatically, but a powerful preacher comes across that way. Conviction, inspiration, and revolution are the order of the day when a preacher is in the house.

No one else has acquired the title on a universal scale like Jonah. History calls him, "The Preacher". God fashioned him, called him, and sent him to face his task. He was a preaching machine. As you know, it took some amazing persuasion by God, but when He arrived in Nineveh, Jonah preached for three solid days. During that time, the entire city was turned upside down. His preaching was so powerful and the results of his ministry so effective, that one hundred and twenty thousand souls were converted. Never in all of history has anything ever happened like that. The poor, the beggars, the rich, the workers in the field, the soldiers, the officials and even the king himself repented at the preaching of Jonah. This preaching was exceptional. Jesus said, **"The men of Nineveh will stand up at the judgment with this generation and condemn it; for they repented at the preaching of Jonah." Mt. 12:41**

What love God had for the people of Nineveh that He would fashion and procure such a preacher just for them. What kind of extra ordinary preacher did Jonah become so that he might orchestrate such a sovereign finish? I can only believe that Jonah's story was a precursor, not just for the death, burial, and resurrection of Christ, but also as a pointer towards the future when the body of Christ will rise to see the glory of God. That will be a time when the nations will burst into flames under the heat of the preachers' fires. I do wish I could have been there to see the amazing sight of Jonah's day, but one day we will see a reenactment. It will happen not just in one nation or one city, but all across America and all around the world the Jonah preachers will rise. With all of our hearts, let us pray! I can hardly wait!

Chapter 6

The Dove

Jonah's Name

Jonah means "dove". How significant is that and what does it mean?

A movie star, rock musician, famous athlete, or TV celebrity, are common choices for naming a newborn in modern, western societies. Their names may sound intriguing, or they may conjure up warm, fuzzy feelings of popular culture or fantasy heroism because they have become famous through the silver screen.

In the Sixties, hippies named their children after the sun, moon or stars, or some earthy tree, moss or bird. Their name choosing might have reflected some form of new age, free spirit euphemism. It seems not too far removed from many native peoples who often named their children after local animals, wind, water, or sky.

Today, in places like Africa, it is common to name a child after a character quality, or a phrase that points to something positive. First names like Splendid, Kindness, Good Luck, Best Choice, and Top Brass have become popular in Africa.

Hundreds of years ago, names were given to highlight one's suggested occupation. Thatcher, Cobbler, Smith, or Farmer identified not only, who a person was, but also told us what they did to make a living.

In ancient times, as with very strong religious or political homes today, newborns are often given the names of a hero of the faith, or a famous political leader from one's nation. Names like Jesus, Mary, Mohammad or Washington, Jackson or Madison are in vogue. In countries like India, where the Hindu religion has many deities, it is common to name a child after one of their gods.

More often than not, we name a child after another family member. If we do not give them a relatives' name as their first name, we may sneak it in as a middle name. There may even be a feeling of obligation to follow such a family naming tradition. It is often a matter of honor and respect.

In the Gospels, when Elizabeth told the crowd that her new son would be called John, it evoked an emotional response worthy of being recorded in scripture.

"On the eighth day they came to circumcise the child, and they were going to name him after his father Zechariah, but his mother spoke up and said, "No! He is to be called John."

They said to her, "There is no one among your relatives who has that name."

Then they made signs to his father, to find out what he would like to name the child." Lk. 1:59-62

It was expected that Elizabeth's baby would be named after a relative and when Elizabeth said no, they did not believe her, so they went over her head. They went to Zechariah, the father. He confirmed that the boy would be called John. The angel had insisted upon it, and they did not want a repeat argument with a powerful angel from heaven.

There is always a reason for giving a certain name to a child. Some parents may say, 'we just liked the sound of that name,' but most have a reason that is stronger than that. Even if the reason is not well accepted by others, it is the choice of the parents. So, a child's name usually reflects a value, or a special emphasis that is dear to the parents.

Jewish Parents

Bible names, consistently, have extremely important meanings. When a preacher studies to prepare a sermon, it is common that he will look up the meaning of the name of the Bible character about whom he will be speaking. They are looking for some spiritual insight that will help them tell the story. They usually discover some meaningful detail because God was always involved in the choosing of the name of a Jewish baby.

The Jewish people believe that a child's name is God-given, and the parents have a spiritual mandate from God to name their child correctly. Many names were changed by God when, it seems, an original name did not carry enough meaning. This was true of Abram, Sarah, Jacob, Simon Peter, Saul of Tarsus, and Joseph, who became Barnabas. Naomi means "pleasant", but after a time of great loss and suffering, she tried to change her name to Mara, which means "bitter one". God did not allow her to do it and, thankfully, her friends did not allow it either.

According to Rabbi Shraga Simmons, "The naming of a Jewish child is a most profound spiritual moment. The Sages say that naming a baby is a statement of her character, her specialness, and her path in life. For at the beginning of life we give a name, and at the end of life a "good name" is all we take with us. Further, the Talmud tells us that parents receive one-sixtieth of prophecy when picking a name. An angel comes to the parents and whispers the Jewish name that the new baby will embody." [ii]

Deeper Meaning

The Rabbi goes on in his explanation: "In Hebrew, a name is not merely a convenient conglomeration of letters. Rather the name reveals its essential character. The Midrash (Genesis Raba 17:4) tells us that the first man, Adam, looked into the essence of every creature and named it accordingly. The donkey, for example, is characterized by carrying heavy, physical burdens. So in Hebrew, the donkey is named "chamor"- from the same root as "chomer", which means materialism. (Contrast this with English, where the word "donkey" doesn't reveal much about the essence of a donkey!)

The same idea applies to the names of people. For example, Leah named her fourth son Judah (in Hebrew, Yehudah). This comes from the same root as the word "thanks." The letters can also be rearranged to spell out the holy Name of God. The significance is that Leah wanted to particularly express her thanks to God." (Genesis 29:35) ." [iii]

The Dove Speaks

Jonah means "dove". With this background and insight into Jewish names, we understand that Jonah was not named "dove" accidentally. God chose this name for this man.

Besides the use of the dove in the romantic literature of Songs of Solomon and the use of the dove as a sacrifice unto God, given by the poor, it is referenced in three significant places.

First of all, the dove was the bird, used by Noah, which brought back an olive leaf and informed those on the ark that the world was alive again (see Genesis 8:8-12). This was an event that marked the end of God's judgment, the extension of peace, and a new beginning for the earth. It has stood as a symbol of peace with God, for all humanity, since that day. This symbolic use of the dove is connected with Jonah, the dove. He was sent by God to

Nineveh to displace the judgment and release the peace of God upon the city.

Secondly, the Holy Spirit descended upon Jesus when He was baptized at the start of his earthly ministry. God spoke in an audible voice at that time.

"As soon as Jesus was baptized, he went up out of the water. At that moment heaven was opened, and he saw the Spirit of God descending like a dove and lighting on him. And a voice from heaven said, "This is my Son, whom I love; with him I am well pleased."" Mt. 3:17

The dove is a symbol of the Holy Spirit, the Holy Spirit anointing, and His manifest presence. Jonah was going to Nineveh under the power of the Holy Spirit. He went with the anointing of the heavenly Dove.

Thirdly, as Jesus was with His disciples, "He asked, **"Who do you say I am?" Simon Peter answered, "You are the Christ, the Son of the living God." Jesus replied, "Blessed are you , Simon son of Jonah, for this was not revealed to you by man, but by my Father in Heaven."** Mt. 16:15-17

Later, in the book of John we read three times, while restoring Peter, Jesus calls him, Simon the son of Jonah. It appears that Peter's father's name was Jonah, but Jesus emphasizes this because Peter was, indeed the son of the dove, the son of the Holy Spirit. God chose Simon Peter to be the son of a man named Jonah. This was not an accident; he was destined to hear from God's Holy Spirit and not just from man. Both in the natural and in the spiritual, Peter was the son of Jonah.

Jonah rightly means dove (the Holy Spirit) because the dove was sent out by Noah, the Holy Spirit has been sent into the world to draw people to repentance, and Jonah was sent in that same Spirit to minister to the people of Nineveh.

America the Dove

The ministry of the dove is also the call of God on America. She has been set aside for ministry, and raised up by God to reach the nations of the world. She is called to do it in the power of the Holy Spirit. In the fullness of time, the church in the USA will minister compassion and mercy to the nations, and in so doing, she will call a dying world to repentance. The day is coming for this great mission, but first God must deal with the sins of America. Then, and only then, will the dove nation, the Jonah nation, arise.

Chapter 7

Nation Forming

This is My Father's World

How was America birthed? From the days of Babel, the birth of nations has been an on-going, consistent directive. Like Adam, the first man, each nation has emerged from the dust of the earth. All of them were made by a decisive, sovereign act of God, yet each is unique, has a specific purpose, and has a life and destiny of its own.

Most nations have had a violent, catastrophic start forced by invading armies, or intruding treasure hunters. Many of those starts were explosive; the nations were birthed like young mountains thrusting and straining upward under the unyielding pressure of colliding tectonic plates. Often, nations known as superpowers decided to created new boundaries and governments, sometimes with just the stroke of a pen. Every time that happened, the local people were inevitably shoved into a struggle for survival. The birth of a nation brings joy for some but usually pain for others.

The world is constantly shifting and, in the process, nations burst forth from the terra firma. Some glisten in the sun with youthful, almost giddy pride, but others come with hanging heads of shame: the consequence of horrific abuse and violence.

Only a few nations were formed by well-intentioned homesteaders looking for a place to settle and work. They entered a new land to live in peace with the nomads who were there and with the environment. They came to work the ground, find a place to raise their families, and develop a good society. Nation building is monumental. It is the stuff of conquerors and greedy treasure seekers, but it is also the stuff of well-meaning pioneers, and settlers. Whoever is coming to build a nation, there is nothing simple or casual about it. Regardless of its well-intentioned or forceful start, it is always catastrophic for someone. Still, all nations come from God. The scripture gives us answers. We begin with the writings of Luke in the book of Acts.

"The God who made the world and everything in it is the Lord of heaven and earth and does not live in temples built by hands. And he is not served by human hands, as if he needed anything, because he himself gives all men life and breath and everything else. From one man he made every nation of men, that they should inhabit the whole earth; and he determined the times set for them and the exact places where they should live. God did this so that men would seek him and perhaps reach out for him, though he is not far from each one of us." Acts 17:24-27

A Sovereign God

It seems that men make nations, but it is God who births them. It is not a simple matter, for He has given all men a free will and therefore He does not determine their personal actions and activities. He gives men the opportunity to be good, then He blesses good and punishes evil. In the process, He guides the steps of those who follow Him, and rewards those who diligently seek Him. There is a tension between the free will of man and the sovereignty of God. Nations emerge as the compassions and judgments of God are released. God is patient and longsuffering, but He has established the laws of sowing and reaping, and in time, He enforces them. He punishes a nation that hurts the innocent or abuses the disadvantaged. When mankind's cup of abuse is full, then the judgments of God follow. Often it results in the death of a nation. Then we see a conquering army rise up to overthrow it.

Following a time of judgment, people may turn from their wicked ways and seek the Lord. God gives fresh opportunities for people who will turn from their evil ways. The Lord says, **"If my people, who are called by my name, will humble themselves and pray and seek my face and turn from their wicked ways, then I will hear from heaven and will forgive their sin and will heal their land." 2 Ch. 14:7**

Like the new earth that emerged after Noah's flood, so a new nation will emerge where an old one stood. In His mercy, God allows people to start over again. Nations are formed and communities have another chance to create a kingdom of integrity and righteousness.

The purpose in the heart of God, always points in one direction; the opportunity for people to find Him, follow His ways, and receive His blessings. As the scripture says, **"God did this**, [creates anew nations], **so that men would seek him and perhaps reach out for him, though he is not far from each one of us." Acts 17:27**

God Reached Out to Native America

In the fullness of time, God made the United States of America. Previously, the huge track of land was sparsely populated by thousands of nomadic tribes. Some were peaceful like the Huron Indians, while others, like the Iroquois tribes, were warmongering and bloodthirsty. When the Europeans arrived they discovered tribes attacking and annihilating entire villages. They enslaved any survivors and owned them as chattel. As on most continents, there was a mixture of good and evil behavior among the indigenous peoples of the Americas.

All of the tribes were deeply religious and some, no doubt, had already been moved upon by their Creator, but the need to know Him in a deeper way was evident. All of the people, whether kindhearted or wicked, were in need of salvation through Jesus Christ. God was preparing to bring the Gospel to them and many of them would open their hearts and receive it. One such example is seen in the work of John Elliot, a Congregational minister. **"Obedient to the New Testament command to preach the Gospel to all nations, ministers in all of the first British North American colonies strove to convert the local native populations to Christianity, often with only modest results. One of the most successful proselytizers was John Elliot (1604-1690) Congregational minister at Roxbury, Massachusetts. His translation of the Bible into the Algonquin Indian language was a success. At one time Elliot ministered to eleven hundred "praying Indians," organized into fourteen New England style towns."** [iv]

Persecuted Believers in Europe

For centuries prior to arriving in America, believers in Europe had suffered unconscionable traumas because of religious persecution. Many of them were looking for a new start away from the tyranny of evil despots. We cannot point a finger at the savage behavior of Indians in the New Land, without also recognizing the extreme depravity of the bloodthirsty Europeans. War, enslavement, torture, the shedding of innocent blood, and extreme religious persecution was every bit as prevalent in England, France, Spain and Germany, as it was in any other part of the world. The majority of early immigrants to The New Americas came for religious freedom. They looked for a place to worship their God free from harassment and persecution.

We read, "Many of the British North American colonies that eventually formed the United States of America were settled in the seventeenth century by men and women, who, in the face of European persecution, refused to compromise passionately held religious convictions and fled Europe. The New England colonies, New Jersey, Pennsylvania, and Maryland were conceived and established "as plantations of religion." Some settlers who arrived in these areas came for secular motives- "to catch fish" as one New Englander put it - but the great majority left Europe to worship God in the way they believed to be correct. They enthusiastically supported the efforts of their leaders to create "a city on a hill," or a "holy experiment," whose success would prove that God's plan for his churches could be successfully realized in the American wilderness. Even colonies like Virginia, which were planned as commercial ventures, were led by entrepreneurs who considered themselves "militant Protestants" and who worked diligently to promote the prosperity of the church."[v] I will address the subject of persecution in Europe in more detail in the next chapter.

God Made America

For many reasons, God made America. He did it for the native people who were already living there and He did it for the faithful who needed freedom from persecution. There was, however, much more in the works. America was made with a special purpose. Her magnificent destiny and calling will one day reach far beyond the dreams of the early men and women of faith who came to her shores. Her greatness began in her founding moments, but much more is coming. God is not finished with America.

Chapter 8

Religious Persecution In Europe

The Evil Stain

Religious persecution was rife throughout Europe prior to 1689 when it was renounced in England as unacceptable. For many more years it continued on the continent and Christians throughout all of Europe dreamed of a new life, free from their tormentors. Murder, torture, public shunning and social restrictions were remained prevalent in many places. In England, even after 1689, the memory of horror from only decades before remained in the minds and stories of spiritual people. They were determined to find religious freedom, no matter the cost. A dark and evil stain had been painted with the brush of religious uniformity and intolerance and it terrified the multitudes. Some thought, it was just a matter of time until the worst atrocities would return. The iron tools of torture could not be forgotten.

Huguenots Butchered

In Burgundy, France, the Huguenots (French Protestants) were killed en masse by Catholics. "The worse was the notorious St. Bartholomew's Day Massacre in Paris, August 24, 1572. Thousands of Huguenots were butchered by Roman Catholics mobs ... perhaps as many as 400,000 French Protestants immigrated to various parts of the world, including the British North American colonies[vi]

In the following paragraphs, I describe several historical engravings and illustrations that depict horrific religious persecutions from the sixteenth and seventeenth centuries. These paragraphs are not for the faint hearted or those sensitive to cruel violence. These brutal events influenced many Europeans to flee their homelands for a better life in British North America. For the sake of their families and communities, they had to get as far away from the carnage as possible. Copies of all of the illustrations I describe are kept in the US Library of Congress in the Rare Book and Special Collections Division.

David van der Leyen

Our first illustration depicts the torture and death of David van der Leyen. He is an example of many Dutch Anabaptists or Mennonites who were murdered by Catholic authorities. His death took place in Ghent in 1554. He was throttled and torched and finally killed as an iron pitch fork was thrust through his bowels. [vii]

John Rogers

The death of John Rogers is depicted in Fox's Book of Martyr's. In the 1530's, he converted to Protestantism from Catholicism. He partnered with William Tyndale in the translation and publication of English Bibles. On

February 4, 1555, after being charged with heresy for his many challenges against the Catholics faith, Rogers was burned alive, at the stake, in the town of Smithfield, England. The orders for his cruel death were given by Queen Mary who was set on forcing everyone in the nation to become Catholic. [viii]

Death by Drowning

One illustration in the Library of Congress shows Protestant believers being killed by Irish Catholics in the year 1641. They were drowned in the River Bann just outside of Portadown, Ulster. Over one hundred Protestants were imprisoned and tortured then herded onto a bridge like cattle. They were stripped naked and forced to jump from the bridge into the water below. Any survivors from the fall were shot. Many women and children were included in the atrocity. [ix]

Catholics Persecuted As Well

It was not just nonconformist Protestants, like Mennonites or Puritans who were persecuted. Mainline Protestants such as Anglicans were persecuted by Catholics, and when they gained political control, the Protestants persecuted and killed Catholics. For example, one illustration in the collection shows the death of the famous Catholic priest, John Olgilvie (olgilby). He was sentenced to death by a Glasgow court in Scotland. On March 10, 1615 he was hung by the neck and his limp body was then mutilated with knives for public display. [x]

Vile Torture Against Catholics

The descriptions in this paragraph are especially diabolical. Cruel, demonic tortures perpetrated against Catholics were just as evil as those instituted by them. The Huguenot Protestants are shown in a series of illustrations committing unheard of carnage. St. Macaire, Gascony, Mans and other towns in France witnessed atrocities around the year 1607. One priest is shown to be cut open and his intestines are wound around a stick and yanked out of him. Another one was buried while still alive. Other pictures show Catholic children being cut to pieces with swords. One illustration shows a priest having his genitals cut away, then cooked and he is forced to eat them. He was then cut open so they could witness him digesting his own private parts. [xi]

Pilgrims and Puritans

In 1620 the Pilgrims landed at Plymouth, Massachusetts. They were Protestant believers who had no faith in the Church of England. They were not expecting to reform the Church; they wanted a complete new start far away from the religion of the monarchy and the state church.

Later, in the 1630s, as many as twenty thousand Puritans arrived in British North America. They were Congregationalists who believed in the Church of England and fought for its reformation, not its annihilation. They thought the Church of England had retained too many of the Catholic trappings. They hoped that the Anglican Church would be cleansed of the papal system, its unbiblical practices and dogma. They expected the Church of England to eventually adopt their New England form of church order. Their hopes were never realized.

Even in the 1630s strong persecution was felt against the Puritans by the English state. This included death threats, torture and imprisonment for many of their members. Because of their religious convictions many had their property taken and were sentenced to life in prison. Others were mutilated having an ear cut off, their nose slit open or an "S.L." branded on their face. It stood for Seditious Liable. It is no wonder that once the way to the Americas opened so many fled Europe for religious freedom.

William Bradford

One of the spiritual leaders on the Mayflower (the second ship of the Pilgrims), was William Bradford. Born in 1590 in Yorkshire, England, Bradford was orphaned at a young age. Although as a boy he lived with various relatives, he was very much a self-made religious man. His fervent love for God grew strong until at age 17, he could not abide the false teachings of the church any longer. As would many of his countrymen, he became a radical. He tried to encourage his congregation to separate from the Church of England and soon he faced threats of harsh persecution from the State. Under the pressure, Bradford fled for his life to Amsterdam, Holland.

At the age of thirty, Bradford planned to be part of a new venture. He would be one of the Pilgrims heading for the New World, a land of religious freedom, across the sea. He struggled with raising adequate finances and he wrestled with the idea of returning to England from where the Mayflower would set sail. Finally, the Government tolerated his departure to the New World, but due to insufficient funds, the ship's company was forced to include non-believers who would help foot the bill. So, believers and non-believers joined together for the journey of their lives.

The Mayflower was 90 feet long and 26 feet at the widest point. One hundred and twenty souls came aboard, including 35 children and several pregnant women. Many were crammed below deck due to the shortage of space. Rough seas, violent storms and a major crack in a main beam brought great fear and concern to the passengers and crew. And almost all of the passengers became wretchedly seasick throughout the journey. Then in November of 1620 a weary Mayflower arrived, shaken but safe, on the wild American coast at Cape Cod.

William's Diary

The following paragraphs have been taken directly from the diary of William Bradford. I have copied some paragraphs and sentences without including the entire section. I think many modern readers would find any diary from this time period too tedious and wordy. A diligent reader can discover William Bradford's complete diary on line, just follow my footnote.

Here are sections of William Bradford diary as they were written in 1630. The quotations begin with Chapter One in his diary. Part way through you will discover that we shift to Chapter 9 and the date September 6 when Bradford begins to record the voyage of the Mayflower.

"It is well known unto the godly ... in our honorable nation of England, what wars and oppositions ... Satan hath raised, maintained and continued against the Saints, from time to time, in one sort or other. Sometimes by bloody death and cruel torments; other whiles imprisonments, banishments and other hard usages.

He [Satan] then began to sow errors, heresies and wonderful dissensions amongst the professors themselves, working upon their pride and ambition, with other corrupt passions.

Mr. Fox recordeth how that besides those worthy martyrs and confessors which were burned in Queen Mary's days and otherwise tormented, "Many (both students and others) fled out of the land to the number of 800, and became several congregations, at Wesel, Frankfort, Basel, Emden, Markpurge, Strasburg, and Geneva, etc. " Amongst whom began the bitter war of contention and persecution about the ceremonies and service book, and other popish and antichristian stuff, the plague of England to this day, which are like the high places in Israel which the prophets cried out against.

The one side labored to have the right worship of God and discipline of Christ established in the church, according to the simplicity of the gospel, without the mixture of men's inventions; and to be ruled by the laws of God's word.

Religion hath been disgraced, the godly grieved, afflicted, persecuted, and many exiled; sundry have lost their lives in prisons and other ways. On the other hand, sin hath been countenanced; ignorance, profaneness and atheism increased, and the papists encouraged to hope again for a day.

This made the holy man Mr. Perkins cry out ...

Religion (saith he) hath been amongst us this thirty-five years; but the more it is published, the more it is contemned and reproached of many, etc. Thus not profanes nor wickedness but religion itself is a byword, a mockingstock, and a matter of reproach; so that in England at this day the man or woman that begins to profess religion and to serve God, must resolve with himself to sustain mocks and injuries.

But after these things they could not long continue in any peaceable condition, but were hunted and persecuted on every side, so as their former afflictions were but as flee-bitings in comparison of these which now came upon them. For some were taken and clapped up in prison, others had their houses beset and watched night and day, and hardly escaped their hands; and most were fain to flee and leave their houses and habitations, and the means of their livelihood.

Yet seeing themselves thus molested, and that there was no hope of their continuance there, by a joint consent they resolved to go into the low Countries, where they heard was freedom of religion for all men.

Chapter 9, September 6.

These troubles being blown over and now all being compact together in one ship, they put to sea again with a prosperous wind which continued diverse days together which was some encouragement unto them; yet according to the usual manner many were afflicted with sea sickness.

After they had enjoyed fair winds and weather for a season, they were encountered many times with cross winds, and met with many fierce storms, with which the ship was shroudly shaken, and her upper works made very leaky; and one of the main beams in the mid ships was bowed and cracked, which put them in some fear that the ship could not be able to perform the voyage.

In all this voyage there died but one of the passengers ... after a long beating at sea they fell with the land which is called Cape Cod; the which being made and certainly known to be it, they were not a little joyful.

Being thus arrived in a good harbor and brought safe to land, they fell upon their knees and blessed the God of heaven, who had brought them over the vast and furious ocean, and delivered them from all the perils and miseries thereof, again to set their feet on the firm and stable earth, their proper element.

May not and ought not the children of these fathers say: "Our fathers were Englishmen which came over this great ocean, and were ready to perish in this wilderness; but they cried unto the Lord, and he heard their voice, and looked on their adversity, etc. Let them therefore praise the Lord, because he is good, and his mercies endure forever. Yea, let them which have been redeemed of the Lord, show how he hath delivered them from the hand of the oppressor. When they wandered in the desert wilderness out of the way, and found no city to dwell in, both hungry, and thirsty, their soul was overwhelmed in them. Let them confess before the Lord his loving kindness, and his wonderful works before the sons of men." [xii]

A Christian Community

It is evident that most of the first settlers who came to British North America came to escape religious persecution. They arrived in the New World with the express purpose of establishing a Christian community. Through extreme hardship and much perseverance they accomplished their goal. Little did they know at the time, how great America would become. Only God had the big picture and the complete plan that was the real reason behind the mission of the Pilgrims. Even today, He alone knows the full extent of America's purpose. Little by little, some have in the past, and some in days to come will discover the immense calling and the magnificent design in the heart of God for America. It will become evident in the church and in time multitudes in the nation and around the world will witness the amazing call of God, the seed of which was planted, in the seventeen hundreds by a boat full of Pilgrims. He is our dwelling place in all generations and He knows the end from the beginning. Let your faith soar and believe for great things.

Chapter 9

The Purpose Of America

The Last-Days Nation

Like Jonah, the USA has an extraordinary destiny. America is what I call, 'God's Last Days Nation'. It was founded by God for His end-time purpose. Here are four godly pillars of purpose for America. I will explain them more extensively in a future chapter.

1. To be a Christian nation.

2. To demonstrate God's love to the world.

3. To spread the Gospel of God's Kingdom, globally.

4. To stand with Israel for God's end-time purpose.

We will look at each of these claims further, but to start with let us recognize that many of the founding fathers of the United States knew some aspects of this prophetic call. Most were wholly Christian and believed that America was founded by God for His sovereign purpose. Their Christian beliefs formed the basis of their philosophies and their understanding of God's purpose for America. Here are some of the thoughts and words of those who forged the USA. The following quotes were taken from an article in the Charlotte Observer, dated July 4, 2009. Printed by Hobby Lobby in association with Wall Builders ministry. It was printed to celebrate America's Independence Day.

The Presidents Speak

- <u>George Washington said</u>, **"It is the duty of all nations to acknowledge the providence of Almighty God, to obey His will, to be grateful for his benefits, and humbly to implore his protection and favor."** George Washington - Commander-in-Chief in the American Revolution; Signer of the Constitution; First president of the United States.

- <u>John Adams wrote</u>, **"Our constitution was made only for a moral and religious people. It is wholly inadequate to the government of any other."** John Adams - Signer of the Declaration of Independence; One of two signers of the Bill of Rights; Second President of the United States.

- <u>Thomas Jefferson wrote</u>, **"And can the liberties of a nation be thought secure when we have removed their only firm basis, a conviction in the minds of the people that these liberties are a gift of God? That they are not to be violated but with His wrath? Indeed I tremble for my country when I reflect that God is just ; that His justice cannot sleep forever."** Thomas Jefferson - Signer and principal author of the Declaration of Independence; Third president of the United States.

- James Madison said, "**Before any man can be considered as a member of civil society, he must be considered as a subject of the Governor of the Universe.**" James Madison - Signer of the Constitution; Fourth president of the United States.

- John Quincy Adams said, "**Is it not that in the chain of human events, the birthday of the nation is indissolubly linked with the birthday of the Savior? … Is it not that the Declaration of Independence first organized the social compact on the foundation of the Redeemer's mission on earth? - That it laid the cornerstone of human government upon the first precepts of Christianity?**" John Quincy Adams - Statesman; Diplomat; Sixth president of the United States.

Influential Leaders Speak

- Benjamin Franklin wrote, "God governs in the affairs of men. If a sparrow cannot fall to the ground without His notice, is it probable that an empire can rise without His aid? We've been assured in the sacred writings that unless the Lord builds the house, they labor in vain who build it. I firmly believe this, and I also believe that without His concurring aid, we shall succeed in this political building no better than the builders of Babel." Benjamin Franklin - Signer of the Declaration of Independence and the Constitution.

- Patrick Henry wrote, "There is a just God who presides over the destinies of nations and who will raise up friends to fight our battles for us … Is life so dear or peace so sweet as to be purchased at the price of chains and slavery? Forbid it Almighty God! I know not what course others may take; but as for me, give me liberty or give me death.!!!" Patrick Henry - Lawyer; Orator; Statesman; Revolutionary Leader (1736 -1799).

- <u>John Jay wrote</u>, " **The Bible is the best of all books, for it is the word of God and teaches us the way to be happy in this world and in the next. Continue therefore to read it and to regulate your life by its precepts. Providence has given to our people the choice of their rulers, and it is the duty, as well as the privilege and interest of our Christian nation, to select and prefer Christians for their rulers."** John Jay - Co-author of the Federalist Papers; First Chief Justice of the U.S. Supreme Court.

- <u>James Wilson wrote</u>, **"Human law must rest its authority ultimately upon the authority of that law which is Divine. ... Far from being rivals or enemies, religion and law are twin sisters, friends, and mutual assistants."** James Wilson - Signer of Declaration of Independence and the Constitution; Original justice on the U.S. Supreme Court.

A Christian Congress Speaks

It was not just influential individuals, such as every early President, who was a person of the Christian faith, it was also Congress as an entity that declared America to be a Christian nation. This sentiment in Congress continued for more than a hundred years after the founding of the nation.

- <u>Senate Judiciary Committee stated</u>, **"We are a Christian people... not because the law demands it, not to gain exclusive benefits or to avoid legal disabilities, but from choice and education; and in a land thus universally Christian, what is to be expected, what desired, but that we shall pay due regard to Christianity."** Senate Judiciary Committee Report, January 19, 1853.

- House Judiciary Committee, "At the time of the adoption of the Constitution and the amendments, the universal sentiment was that Christianity should be encouraged ... there can be no substitute for Christianity ... That was the religion of the founders of the republic and they expected it to remain the religion of their descendants." House Judiciary Committee Report, March 27, 1854.

The Universities Speak

Even the places of higher learning in the New America were completely Christian in motive and expression. Both Harvard and Yale Universities were founded and developed for Christian education. Their Christian guidelines were seen as the only correct model for science and life skill. We read some of their early statements such as these guidelines for students.

- Harvard University Student Guidelines, "Let every student be plainly instructed and earnestly pressed to consider well the main end of his life and studies is to know God and Jesus Christ which is eternal life (John 17:3) and therefore to lay Christ in the bottom as the only foundation of all sound knowledge and learning. And seeing the Lord only giveth wisdom, let every one seriously set himself by prayer in secret to seek it of Him (Proverbs 2,3) Every one shall so exercise himself in reading the scriptures twice a day that he shall be ready to give such an account of his proficiency therein." Harvard University; 1636 Guidelines.

- Yale University Student Guidelines, "All the scholars are required to live a religious and blameless life according to the rules of God's word, diligently reading the Holy Scriptures, that fountain of Divine light and truth, and constantly attending all the duties of religion." Yale University; 1787 Guidelines.

The United States was founded by God to be a Christian nation, with a Judeo-Christian standard of morality and behavior. Even though it had and has serious faults, the founders walked with God and He walked with them. This is God's nation, designed by Him for a special end-time purpose.

Think of how God has used America. Already the United States has sent out more missionaries, given more money to help the poor, and has stood with Israel, more than any other nation in history.

America has, although with slanderous intent, been called the policeman of the world. This, however, is an honorable title, not a derogatory one. Policemen who do their job, are good; they protect the innocent and apprehend the wicked. Oppressed people around the world, cry for America's help. I thank God for all that the United States of America does to fulfill her calling.

Get ready to see more of these things in the future. America's finest days are still ahead of her. She will fulfill her God-given destiny.

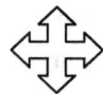

Chapter 10

Exceptionalism In America

A Premise for Greatness

In this chapter we will look, for a moment, at America's exceptionalism. This topic deserves a book of its own, but for our purposes, a few chapters will suffice. In a previous chapter titled, 'The Purpose of America', I highlighted four dynamics that I believe are a partial list that describe God's purpose and call for America.

These dynamics include:

1. To be a Christian nation.

2. To demonstrate God's love to the world.

3. To spread the Gospel of God's Kingdom, globally.

4. To stand with and bless Israel for God's end-time purpose.

To explain the premise of American exceptionalism, we must look at some of the great things already accomplished by the government and citizens of the USA. It is not to say that other nations are not exceptional in their own way, but that America is in her own way. She is a leader in the world. It is easy to criticize a leader especially when there is a mixture of good and bad in one's performance, nevertheless, the facts of exceptional behavior in America remain.

Egalitarianism

Egalitarianism would say that all nations are equal in every way, but no nation is the same as any other, just like people are not the same. When it comes to salvation and the spiritual benefits of God's grace, the Creator is not a respecter of persons (Acts 10:34). He does not exclude anyone from being blessed in His ocean of kindness. God is not racist, in fact, He abhors racism. All people are made in the image of God and each has a special calling (Genesis 1:27). And He wishes that none would perish, but that all would come to eternal life (2 Peter 3:9). Scripture states there is no difference between male or female, Jew or gentile, slave or free; all are equal in Christ (Galatians 3:28-29). This, equality, however, is regarding salvation and not purpose. For example; there is an obvious difference between male and female when it comes to roles and purpose, but not when it comes to salvation. No man that I know of has birthed a child, men and women are very different in many ways.

Some will have a different role to play and some may even be called to a greater purpose than others. Israel and the Jewish people have a very special calling. They were chosen by God for an eternal purpose even before one of them was born.

Moses had a predetermined calling on his life. He was protected from birth because he had a job to fulfill. Joseph, one of the twelve sons of Jacob, did as well; he had a higher calling than his brothers. God gave him dreams to inform him of his special grace. David was chosen by God form the very start. God assigned him to be the king of Israel and to be a foreshadow of the greatest of all kings. Jesus was king then, and forever will be the king of the whole world.

People are often jealous when one is called to greatness. We saw it with the jealousies of Miriam and Aaron, the sister and brother of Moses. God almost killed them because they claimed egalitarianism. Also, because of jealousy, David was mocked and put down by his brothers, and Joseph with his coat of many colors, was almost killed by his.

It is not easy being destined for greatness. We certainly found that to be true for Jonah. As we look at the USA, we discover a nation that is mocked and judged harshly by many others in the world, but her special calling remains.

Moses, Joseph, David, Mary or Paul did nothing so great as to deserve the unusual purpose that each of them was given. Certainly the Jews have not deserved the promise of blessings and purpose that are coming to them. They could not boast because of something they did to deserve the greatness they are afforded. In fact, the Bible tells us that they failed seriously, on numerous accounts. In many ways America has failed also; she does not deserve the special calling that is laid up for her.

Extraordinary greatness is coming to America and with greatness comes great responsibility. One day it must be acted upon and fulfilled. A calling, belongs to the one to whom it was given. When discovered, it can be painful, for greatness in the end, comes at a great price.

There is another reason, besides predetermination, for the initiation of a special call to greatness from the Lord. It is found in the law of sowing and reaping. Exodus twenty, verses four and five are part of the famous Ten Commandments. They declare that God will punish families for the idol worship of a father, and likewise will bless families whose ancestors have loved God with distinction. Greatness and a special calling can therefore come upon a child because of their own love for God, or because of the extraordinary godly activities, prayers and love of their parents or grandparents.

A Christian Nation

In the previous chapters we highlighted some of the facts that point to America being designed by God as a Christian nation. The Pilgrims came with this purpose and many of the first presidents and other founding fathers echoed that sentiment. I understand that it is highly contested by some, but I think it is clear. I am not alone in stating that this country was founded on biblical principles and that many of its founders framed it to be a Christian nation.

It is evident in the scriptures that some nations will enter the Messianic millennium, which will be under the direct rule of King Jesus. With all that has transpired in America's birth process and her ongoing biblical exceptionalism, it is obvious to me, that she will be one of those nations. The United States of America will one day be a full-blown Christian nation. While governments may wander far from this premise, the people will one day turn to God, and see this nation redeemed and she will fulfill her calling and purpose.

The evidence of America's Christian roots, are undeniable, but who can know the mind of God regarding the future, unless God reveals it? So we leave the fact that America was founded to be a Christian nation, as it stands and we move on. I trust that many of you reading this book agree with me on this first point.

Demonstrating God's Love to the World

Let us look at our second point; America is called to demonstrate God's love to the world. In 2012, the USA gave $31.2 billion for economic add to other nations. *"Military aid is about a third of all foreign aid. The remaining two thirds is categorized as economic assistance.*

The top five economic assistance categories in 2012 included global health and child survival, international narcotics control and law enforcement, and migration and refugee assistance. Other programs in the economic assistance category include the Peace Corps, international disaster and famine assistance, and disease control through the Centers for Disease Control." [xiii]

I will leave the spreading of the gospel and blessing Israel to future chapters although they are also included in this theme of loving the world. It is time to take a brief look at America's humanitarian efforts that involve providing food, water, clothes and shelter for the poor of the world. This is amazing.

In the next chapter, we will also recognize America's efforts to protect and rescue the down trodden and oppressed people in tyrannical regimes around the world and those hit by severe natural disasters. They are also an expression of demonstrating God's love to the world.

Humanitarian Efforts Up Close

I have travelled to more than 45 nations around the world preaching the Gospel and have often seen the humanitarian aid that has come to other nations from the USA. Whether in Haiti, Burundi, Guatemala or dozens of other nations, I have seen first-hand the distribution of U.S. food to the poor. For years after the tragic genocide in Rwanda and Burundi, thousands of women were widowed and many more children were orphaned. The economy of those nations was decimated and millions of people were facing the threat of starvation. I travelled with a church team to a refugee camp in Burundi to help distribute the bags of US grits to the hungry. They lined up for hours as bags with the label USA were opened and the women and children were fed. Wherever we have gone around the world we have seen it. A large percentage of food and finances have come from the US government so that the displaced that were hungry could be fed. The U.S. is exceptional.

Humanitarian Facts

The following statistics were taken from the Global Humanitarian Assistance website. [xiv]

Here is a record of the amounts of money for 2013 for humanitarian assistance going to other nations from the USA.

Total US government provided humanitarian aid for 2013 totaled $4.7 billion.

Here are some Key Figures:

1. In 2013, the US provided $4.7 billion for humanitarian emergencies, making it the largest government donor of official humanitarian assistance in the world.

2. Over the past decade the US has been the largest government provider of humanitarian assistance. The annual humanitarian assistance increased by 18% in 2013.

3. Over the past decade annual humanitarian assistance has accounted for between 12.9% and 16% 0f the US official development assistance (ODA). In 2013, the US ODA was equal to 0.2% of gross national income (GN)

4. Fifty-nine percent of the US' overall humanitarian assistance in the last ten years has gone to countries in sub-Saharan Africa. The largest recipients of its humanitarian assistance have been Sudan ($4.6 billion), Ethiopia ($3.1 billion) and Pakistan ($1.7 billion). The US was the largest donor to both Ethiopia and Pakistan in 2012.

5. In 2013, the US provided $548 million to the Syria Regional Refugee Response Plan (RRP) appeal, accounting for 25% of all funding.

6. Ninety percent of the US' humanitarian assistance between 2008 and 2012 went to countries classified as fragile in the 2014 OECD Fragile States report.

7. Seventy-nine percent of the US' official humanitarian assistance was spent in countries classified as long-term recipients of humanitarian assistance in 2012.

The USAID Policy Framework 2011-2015 is the first of its kind ... and outlines the United States Agency for International Development (USAID)'s seven core development objectives:

1. Increase food security

2. Promote global health and health systems

3. Reduce climate change impacts and promote low-emissions growth

4. Promote sustainable, broad-based economic growth

5. Expand and sustain the ranks of stable, prosperous and democratic states

6. Provide humanitarian assistance - paying close attention to the challenges women and girls face in post-disaster environments, including the increased risk of sexual violence

7. Support disaster mitigation and prevent and respond to crisis, conflict and instability

That list is valiant focus of kindness and care . Here is a list of the nations that have received the largest amounts of humanitarian aid from the US government between 2003 and 2012. They are only listed here if they were one of the top ten recipients for any year during this time period. The world is a large place and the needs are enormous in so many different nations. The USA, more than any other country has stepped up to help the needy. Here are the main nations they have helped.

Ethiopia

Sudan

Sudan South

Pakistan

Afghanistan

Iraq

West Bank & Gaza Strip

Lebanon

Haiti

Eritrea

Indonesia

Mali

Burundi

Sierra Leon

Liberia

Zimbabwe

Korea Dem. Rep.

Congo Dem. Rep.

Uganda

Kenya

Chad

Somalia

Myanmar

Niger

Sri Lanka

Where the Need Is

The above list is by no means a complete list. It is simply listing the nations who have received the largest amount of aid from the USA. Please notice that the US government aid money was given where the crisis has been most severe. As noted in the above list the Muslim peoples have benefitted from this humanitarian aid more than any other people group. This is because the need has been most severe among these people. The giving of financial aid for food is not dependent on any racial or religious disposition. It has been given to people who have the greatest needs. This is a biblical mandate.

There is always more that can be done, but I am glad that the USA has done what it has done so far. I know in days to come, the USA will do much more.

Citizens Also Give

For those with strong Evangelical church affiliations, it is common knowledge, that the citizens of the USA are also givers to help the poor of other nations. Most of this giving is generated and promoted by evangelical Christians who live in the USA. Their individual giving is championed by mission groups such as Samaritans Purse, the 700 Club led by Pat Robinson, and the efforts of the Billy Graham Association. Thousands of churches raise funds and their members give millions individually.

Financial aid to help feed the poor around the world does not only come from the US government, a huge amount comes from private donors. The USA, its people, and its churches need to rise higher in their giving. They will in days to come. They will fulfill the call of God that rests upon them. The seeds of this focus of giving are already evident.

Only the Beginning of Exceptionalism

American is a nation of giving people; the United States is exceptional. We will continue to discuss America as an exceptional nation in the next few chapters. We will look at America's exceptional freedom, America's exceptional defense for disadvantaged people, America's exceptional missionary efforts around the world, American's exceptional humanitarian aid to the poor, America's exceptional financial opportunities, and America's exceptional stand with Israel. These and other, qualities are those the Bible tells us, please God, and releases His blessings upon a people.

So much can be shown to make the point of American's exceptionalism. It deserves a book of its own, but for our purpose, it can only occupy a few chapters in this one.

It is apparent that some resist the truth of American exceptionalism. I trust the amazing statistics and overview of these chapters will begin to shift that thinking. When we compare America to the rest of the nations, she is overwhelmingly extraordinary; she is exceptional.

Chapter 11

Exceptional Freedom

Freedom for All

No other nation has focused so much on freedom like the USA. It is exceptional. No matter what their ideology or persuasion, the people of America want to be free, and they want everyone else around the world to be free, as well.

Our founding fathers came to these shores to find freedom. They attempted to build a land of religious freedom, economic freedom, and freedom of civil rights. They fought for freedom from tyranny, freedom from poverty, freedom of speech, and freedom to worship according to one's conscience.

Europeans worked hard and found that freedom early on. They preached it and enjoyed it, but it took a long time, and a lot of blood was shed, before the American freedom dream was extended to all who lived here. Racial freedom was sharply resisted, and many believe that America has still not fully attained it.

As I write, large protests are being held in several U.S. cities, under the theme, "Black Lives Matter." Some believe this phrase has been used to say that other lives do not matter. The fact is that all lives matter. Regardless of the inappropriate distortion, many people feel that black people are still oppressed by racial discrimination, and are still being abused in the United States.

Martin Luther King spoke out, in his day of great trouble, and said:

"I say to you that our goal is freedom, and I believe we are going to get there because, however much she strays away from it, the goal of America is freedom. Abused and scorned though we may be as a people, our destiny is tied up in the destiny of America" - Martin Luther King

No matter what perspective people hold regarding racism in America today, non can deny that we have come a long way toward equality, and that the vast majority of people are working hard to achieve and hold onto freedom at every level.

Philosophically, America is 'the land of the Free and the home of the Brave', but it seems that some individuals need to be reminded of it.

Let Freedom Reign

America is a land where one law is for all people, regardless of color, financial means, or social influence. That is the goal and the plan; it is the law of the land, and the constant fight of the people. If it is ever discovered that this law is violated, the entire country will not rest until it is put right. Equality and freedom are the American dream. It is our persuasion and the focus of almost all who live here.

The United States was the first nation in the world to reach for this freedom and today, most Americans enjoy what so many have fought for. Around the world, America is famous, because she is the land of freedom.

In others nations, many freedoms that we take for granted, are completely absent. It is horrifying to think of being accused of a crime in some countries like Iran or China. People are incarcerated and the outcome of their trial may be totally unjust. Many people are not given a fair trial.

Tourists and workers in Iran, for example, have been put in prison, without good reason. Even on the news today, I saw a U.S. journalist is being held without just cause. There is no true freedom in that nation, and Iran is only one of dozens of nations that do not extend personal freedom to the people who live there. It would be a living nightmare, to be put in one of their jails.

In the USA, the worst criminals, terrorists and enemies of the state, are given a fair trial. Their trial may even extend over a long period of time, and costs the U.S. tax payer, millions of dollars, to ensure that justice is being served. Procedures and protocol protect every person, and that is exceptional freedom.

Amazing Freedom

Freedom means different things to different people. To some, it means no slavery. For many folks, who come from other nations, it is the opportunity to pursue a life ambition; one, they could only dream about in their homeland.

Freedom, for some, is the right to work hard, earn a living and to spend their money as they wish. Freedom means one may be their own boss, and not have to come or go at another's leave.

Freedom means a person can marry someone they love, instead of being forced to marry a person they do not love, who has been chosen for them. And, if they are abused in that marriage, they have the freedom in America to leave that abusive partner. Freedoms like this are not available in many nations.

In short, freedom means, a person has the right to live their life the way they want to, as long as it does not hurt another. That is the dream that America pioneered and it is exceptional.

Definitions of Freedom

Nina Simone, the famous singer and activist of the sixties said, "**Freedom is having no fear.**" That became a defining word for Nina. It was a powerful revelation and she reached for it and claimed it.

There are fears within and fears without, but real freedom will exclude both. Fears without, may include; a fear of people, tyranny, wild beasts, poverty, abuse, or oppression.

Fears within, may include; a fear of failure, ill health, rejection, loneliness, and fear of death. A nation and its culture can provide security from fears without, but only God gives freedom from the fears within. Those who walk as disciples of Jesus can know freedom from every fear.

Norman Rockwell created four famous American paintings on this subject. They are called, "The Four Freedoms". They tell the story of what America has done to become the land of the free. The four paintings are titled; "Freedom of Speech", "Freedom of Worship", "Freedom from Want", and "Freedom from Fear".

America is not the only nation that embraces these freedoms, but she was the first, and is by far, the greatest promoter of these freedoms around the world.

Economic Freedom

While religious freedom was a main motivating force that brought people to America hundreds of years ago, economic freedom, is the modern day incentive. Poverty is a curse and America has the antidote. It is possible for everyone in America to be free of poverty. America is the land of opportunity and that is exceptional.

Everywhere I travel, people around the world ask me if I can help them move to America. It seems that the whole world wants to live in America, even those who hate her ideology. The reason is obvious, America is the land of financial opportunity.

No national economic system is perfect, but in the United States, any healthy person, who sets their hearts and hands to train and work hard, can make a good living. If they are wise, and have a good work ethic, they may even become rich. There is no other place on the planet that compares with the financial opportunities, of the USA.

Capitalism, while not perfect, has allowed for massive sums of money to be spread around. Every ethnic group has participated in this success story. People of every color and creed have become wealthy in the USA. There is far more financial fluidity here in America than in any other country, or with any other financial system.

Even though there are many poor black people in the USA, there are still way more rich black people in this country than in any other nation, including the nations where the people are almost exclusively black. This is also true for Hispanics. It is true for people who have come from Eastern Europe, and from almost every other nation and continent. America is a land of economic freedom and that freedom is available to all people groups.

The people of developing nations know the horrors of poverty in their homeland, and multitudes are flocking to America because of it. Let us be truthful, this financial freedom is more than exceptional, it is a global phenomena of our time.

Taxation

Hundreds of years ago a battle was raging over America. The cry of the people back then was, "No taxation without representation!" Now, in America, no citizen is taxed without representation. Furthermore, if a person votes but is not part of the winning ticket, or if the taxes are too high, they can move to an area of the country that they find more favorable. They can find a part of the country with less taxes, and more suitable politics. This is a land of amazing freedom.

The economic freedoms in America are outstanding and should not be overlooked or understated. Nowhere in the world is freedom more alive than in America. This freedom does not guarantee financial security or a good standard of living for everyone, but it provides the opportunity for everyone to find financial security and have a good standard of living.

My Definition

In my role as a pastor, I have consistently taught that **"freedom is the ability to do everything that God wants you to do. It is when you are not held back from doing God's will, for any reason. "**

If you cannot do something that God wants you to do, then you are not free. I argue that a Christian really does not have the freedom to do things contrary to God's will.

Peter Marshall said it like this: ***"May we think of freedom, not as the right to do as we please, but as the opportunity to do what is right."***

I am Wrong

Considering the full definition of freedom, I know my definition is wrong. My definition of freedom is drastically incomplete. Freedom before God, and in the USA, is much larger then my definition. It includes the right, to do things that God does not want a person to do, as well.

A person has a free choice to live in sin, or in a manner that goes against the mainstream ideology of American. As long as a person does not hurt another person, they can do things that others believe to be wrong. That is American freedom; it is exceptional.

Free Speech

America maintains the right of free speech for all who walk the land, citizens and visitors. Those who speak out cannot participate in a hate crime, but they are free to say just about anything else. The government protects this freedom even when a voice is speaking against it, or when a person's ideology goes against that of the populous.

One individual has the freedom to speak in such a way as to go against everyone else in the land, and America will protect and defend them, while they are doing it. That person is free to express themselves even when the government and the people of America find the message offensive.

In many other nations, people who try to speak their minds are imprisoned, tortured, or killed, but not in America. It boasts over its freedom of speech and defends it rigorously.

Don't Mess with America's Freedom

Woodrow Wilson admitted that financial gain was important in America, but our freedom of rights was more important. He said:

"America is not a mere body of traders, it is a body of free men. Our greatness- built upon freedom - is moral, not material, we have a great ardor for gain; but we have a deep passion for the rights of man." - Woodrow Wilson

Ronald Reagan said:

"If we lose freedom here, there is no place to escape to. This is the Last Stand on Earth." Ronald Reagan

Dreaming of coming to America from oppressive Russia, the famous comedian, Yakov Smirnoff said:

"My father described this tall lady who stands in the middle of the New York harbor, holding high a torch to welcome people seeking freedom in America. I instantly fell in love." Yakov Smirnoff

J.F. Kennedy said:

"Let every nation know, whether it wishes us well or ill, we shall pay any price, bear any burden, meet any hardship, support any friend, oppose any foe, to assure the survival and success of liberty [freedom]." J.F. Kennedy

Here are some other famous quotes that highlight America's exceptional freedom.

"Those who deny freedom to others deserve it not for themselves." Abraham Lincoln

"Freedom is what America means to the world." Audie Murphy

"The American flag is the most recognized symbol of freedom and democracy in the world." Virginia Foxx

"We hold these truths to be self-evident, that all men are created equal; that they are endowed by their Creator with certain unalienable rights, that among these, Life, Liberty and the Pursuit of happiness." U.S. Declaration of Independence

Future Freedom

I am amazed at America's focus, fame, and insistence on freedom, and I acknowledge it to be absolutely exceptional, but I know that greater freedom will yet come.

The Bible says, **"Now, the Lord is the Spirit and where the Spirit of the Lord is, there is freedom." 2 Cor.3:17**

The destiny and calling on America channels her future toward the purposes of God. Real freedom cannot be contained or fully know because of the policies or laws of a nation. It is an impartation of God's grace. One day America will know freedom, in its fullness. It will flourish within its borders and within the hearts of her people.

Chapter 12

America - The Hero Nation

The Heroes are Coming

"Shortly after independence from Britain, the United States Navy fought the Barbary War (1801-05). And in 1813, Washington seized its first permanent overseas military base - in the South Pacific island of Nukahiva. Two centuries later, the United States has over 700 bases in 130 countries and spends more on its military budget than the rest of the world combined." [xv]

Although some see this as a negative, I am impressed with the purpose and scope of this initiative. Many others are proud of the USA and its military endeavors as well. I am sure this includes most who serve in the military and millions of every-day American citizens who are grateful for what the US military does at home and around the world. No person, in their right mind, wants war or military strongholds around the world, but most understand that, at times, it is a necessity.

I recognize America's amazing efforts to protect and rescue the down trodden and oppressed people who live under the control of tyrannical regimes. I also agree with the USA being available to help the world when the disadvantaged and poor people are hit by natural disasters. Both of these endeavors are an expression of demonstrating God's love to the world. If the USA has the power to guard or rescue the defenseless or to help those who are dying, should they not do it? Of course they should; the US cannot solve most of the problems around the world, but to try to do what they can is righteous and godly. It is exceptional behavior.

To stand by and watch other humans die when we can prevent it is heartless and sinful. The USA has been blamed for trying to help the poor from the oppression of tyrannical rulers and murderers. The truth is that many times they have stood back, refusing to intervene. People in other lands have cried out to the American government for help and no answer has been given. If anything, the USA is guilty of not doing enough. Nevertheless, compared to all other nations, I have to say that America is a hero nation. So many times she has intervened, and for this we must give her credit.

Comments From the Rescued

I have copied testimonies from various individuals who wish to thank the people and government of the United States for coming and rescuing their nation, or someone else's nation, from evil rulers or foreign These comments are taken from: http://www.quora.com/What-are-some-examples-of-countries-that-have-benefited-from-a-US-military-intervention

The various comments are given in answer to the question -

"What are some examples of countries that have benefited from a US military intervention?"

1. **Anonymous**: This topic is a personal one for me, so I'll dive in. On June 25th, 1950, North Korean forces, supported by China and Russia, invaded

the Republic of Korea (South Korea). United Nations forces, led primarily by the United States, organized a defense and fought three years until an armistice was signed.

From a personal perspective, three of my grandparents came from areas now within North Korea, and fled south after liberation from Japan. My parents came to the United States in the 70s. I can't speak for most Koreans, or even most Korean-Americans, but despite the boneheaded things many Americans say or do, the USA prevented my family from being massacred and is the country I was born to, so you're not going to be hearing me say anything anti-American. If any Koreans I grew up with did, I'm quite sure he got an immediate beating from his parents.

2. **Muhammed Munther**: - Iraqi Kurdistan. We were oppressed, executed by the hundreds, faced chemical attacks, and prevented from exercising our independence.

People were poor and health care was bad. No matter how hard our Kurdish leaders fought for independence and the rights of the Kurdish people, they were faced with a cruel and crazy tyrant who did not hesitate to use chemical attacks to suppress his own people.

The US got rid of Saddam for us and gave us the opportunity to build and prosper.

3. **Jaap Weel**: My home town in the Netherlands was liberated from the Nazis by the 67th Armor, on the 18th of September, 1944. To this day, every last grave at the local American military cemetery is _"adopted" by a Dutch family_ that lays flowers and the like. (And it's a big cemetery, on account of the Battle of the Bulge.)

There is no question that the vast, overwhelming majority of Dutch people are grateful for the American (and British, Canadian, and Polish) soldiers who liberated our country and reinstated civilian, democratic government as soon as possible.

4. **Mike Holovacs**: AA and BA in History. I would argue that Kuwait stands as a good example of a beneficiary. If the Coalition had not stopped Saddam, Kuwait may have become a 1990's version of 1930's Poland where the country simply ceased to exist on a map.

5. **Scott M. Stolz**: History Buff . Studied Political Science. There are many examples. Here are some that comes to mind:

Haiti - On September 30, 1991, a military coup under the leadership of Lieutenant General Raoul Cedras overthrew the government of Jean-Bertrand Aristide, the first popularly elected president in Haitian history. The U.S. eventually intervened with military force, and Cedras capitulated before the troops arrived and the U.S. helped negotiate a transition of power back to a democratically elected government.

Europe & Japan - The United States intervened during World War II and then implemented the Marshal Plan that rebuilt Europe after World War II. After World War I, the winners severely punished the losers of the war, which arguably caused World War II. The Americans proposed and implemented a plan to rebuild Europe, including the losers of the war, so that we wouldn't have a repeat of what happened. Similarly we rebuilt Japan after defeating it in World War II, and it has become one of our strongest allies and an economic powerhouse.

6. **Bojan Zivkovic**: Serbia (then Yugoslavia) in 1999. It was not US only intervention, it was NATO bombing. Yugoslavia during the 90's was ruled by dictator Slobodan Milosevic. Back then, Kosovo was part of Serbia (which was part of Yugoslavia) and was mostly populated by people of Albanian nationality. As such, Kosovo was held by Yugoslavian army and numerous war crimes were committed during that time. NATO bombing put an end to that but also increased Milosevic's unpopularity among people. That directly lead to his overthrow next year.

7. **Scott Workinger**: I met a Croatian graduate student at Stanford who was very appreciative of the US role in stabilizing the situation in the Balkans when Yugoslavia came apart. In the US, at the time, our involvement was controversial.

8. **Chris Davis**: Handyman, Father, Coach, Engineer. Well, hopefully Nigeria, and more than 300 young girls, are about to benefit from our "intervention." The extremists on the left would probably say we shouldn't get involved.[Girls were kidnapped by the fanatical, Islamic, militant faction called Boko Haram]

9. **Anonymous:** The United States prevented Communist China from taking over Taiwan. This saved Taiwan from Mao's madness. To this day the United States prevents China from using aggression on Taiwan.

10. **Eric Moore**: Security Contractor, History Buff. Lebanon in the 50's we sent 15,000 troops there to restore order.

11. **Ron Schmolle**: Cuba in 1898: Spanish elites treated Cubans as if slaves; kept in compounds.

12. **David Tuffley**: Without US military intervention in WW2, Australia would have stood alone against the advancing Japanese Imperial forces that had already taken all of Western Pacific and had arrived on Australia's doorstep. Britain had its hands full in Europe and were no help. Without the US, we could not have withstood the onslaught. Thanks US, you've been a good friend.

13. **Steve Gregg**: Western Europe is free and prosperous due to American military intervention. The Pacific Ocean and all the nations that are in it and line it have benefited from America making it its lake and ensuring commerce can freely flow there.

14. **Hi! I'm just someone loving life:** After reading only half of the responses for the question, I had to stop. I admit I was in tears. I am a P.O.W's daughter. My father, a great man, that loved his family and

country, died from serving this great nation in hopes of liberating anther. He gave his life to save the people of another country. Not just my father, but my uncle, grandfather, and great grandfather. All died either in active duty or from complications from serving in the war.

Hearing all of these wonderful stories of how the USA has helped to enhance others' countries, from a civilians (the people) point of view, makes their (USA Troops) greatest sacrifice (their life) worth it. They Gave Their Life So Others Can Stand And Live A Better Life. (Tears are streaming sorry) It really hits home when you hear stories such as these, it helps to restore pride in my nation. We "the people" mostly hear the news media propaganda and sometimes the waters get murky and the people are misled. We "the people" need to hear from "YOU The People". It truly restores our pride and helps to let us know that our sacrifice was indeed worth it.

15. **Adam Smith**: As an American, it would be rude and inappropriate for me to answer what others should feel about our interventions in their countries. But it was touching to read some of the replies from people in those nations. Most Americans don't fit the stereotype of arrogant thugs who think we do no wrong. After the George W Bush years and the Iraq War, all we hear is how hated and stupid we are. I think we could all use a reminder about the good things we have done, so maybe we can act more like those days and less like the worst things we've done. And I'm not just talking about Americans; that's a universal need.

US Aid for Natural Disasters

Sng Kok Joon Leonard: The US Navy is so omnipresent around the globe, they tend to be one of the first to attend to disasters such as Typhoon Haiyan and the Indian Ocean Tsunami, in addition to having the wherewithal to provide support to remote areas affected.

This too, is US military intervention, and the scope of their involvement in such humanitarian aid by far exceeds their involvement in the ... [negativity] that appears on the news.

The US Navy is also an active participant in counter-piracy across the major sea routes traversing the globe. Technically every country that ships anything anywhere benefits from their 'military intervention.

Here are some recent statistics regarding USA relief services to other nations. [xvi]

"The Office of U.S. Foreign Disaster Assistance (OFDA) is responsible for leading and coordinating the U.S. Government's response to disasters overseas.

OFDA responds to an average of 70 disasters in 56 countries every year to ensure aid reaches people affected by rapid on-set disasters—such as earthquakes, volcanoes, and floods—and slow-onset crises, including drought and conflict. OFDA fulfills its mandate of saving lives, alleviating human suffering, and reducing the social and economic impact of disasters worldwide in partnership with USAID functional and regional bureaus and other U.S. Government agencies.

Our Work

OFDA experts worldwide and in D.C. help countries **prepare** for, **respond to, and recover** from humanitarian crises. OFDA works with the international humanitarian community to give vulnerable populations resources to build resilience and strengthen their own ability to respond to emergencies.

Emergency Response

When disaster strikes, OFDA sends regional and **technical experts** to the affected country to identify and prioritize humanitarian needs. In the wake of a large-scale disaster, OFDA can deploy a Disaster Assistance Response

Team (DART) to coordinate and manage an optimal U.S. Government response, while working closely with local officials, the international community, and relief agencies. OFDA also maintains stocks of emergency relief supplies in warehouses worldwide and has the logistical and operational capabilities to deliver them quickly.

Major world events drove OFDA's actions in FY 2012. In Syria, where more than one million people fled their homes because of escalating violence, OFDA and others in the U.S. Government are responding to growing humanitarian needs in the country and throughout the region.

While conditions in the **Horn of Africa** have improved since 2011 when the worst drought in more than 60 years—combined with ongoing conflict in Somalia—devastated the region, millions still require assistance. As of September 2012, OFDA provided life-saving health assistance to more than 2 million people and increased access to safe drinking water and sanitation facilities for more than 1.7 million people.

In the **West African Sahel**, below-average rainfall and resulting crop losses left people without sufficient food or income. OFDA provided seeds, tools, and agricultural training to more than 660,000 farmers, and prevented and treated malnutrition in nearly 790,000 women and children.

Throughout Asia and Latin America, OFDA responded to flooding in 15 countries, including **Thailand**, **India**, the **Philippines**, **Guatemala**, and **Paraguay**, providing shelter and critical relief supplies to families who lost everything.

Following the deadly 2004 earthquake and tsunami, the people of Indonesia—with financial and technical support from OFDA—developed a tsunami early warning and evacuation system that got people out of harm's way when a magnitude 8.6 earthquake struck off the island of Sumatra in April 2012. Also, early warning systems and disaster preparedness activities established by OFDA in Mozambique saved lives following severe storms and flooding in January 2012.

Early Recovery

Recognizing the need to provide immediate relief while also **setting the stage for recovery and rehabilitation**, OFDA supports programs that give people tools to restart former jobs, provide psychosocial care to traumatized disaster survivors, and prepare individuals to get back on their feet.

OFDA programs also seek innovative ways to help disaster-affected communities begin to rebuild local economies. In many African nations, OFDA provides mobile cash transfers, allowing people to purchase food or other items to restart small businesses, playing a direct role in helping local businesses and farmers recover. Such programs help build resilience, they also protect hard-won economic and development gains."

Is The USA Exceptional?

I have to answer the question, **'Is the USA exceptional?'** with a hearty yes, yes, yes!!

The more I research and discover all that the US government and her citizens do to help others around the world, the more I am convinced that the USA is an exceptional nation. This is all the more true when I compare the USA, and her sacrificial giving, with that of all other nations combined. She far exceeds them.

Her military help around the world is outstanding. I have not even reported the statistics that tell of the massive number of lives (that number in the hundreds of thousands) that have been lost by US soldiers, as they fought to rescue people of other nations.

People at home and abroad do not speak highly enough of America's disaster relief aid programs. These efforts reach far beyond her own doorstep, and it seems, is usually taken for granted .

There is always more that can be done and I believe more will come in time, but already the USA has proven herself to be exceptional in my eyes.

An Act of God

America helps so many around the world in so many extraordinary ways. I understand this position of privilege to be an act of God. It is America's calling; it is America's destiny.

Chapter 13

America's Missionaries

Effective Mission Work is Tough

The Evangelical Christians that I know would love to see the world come to Christ. Whether or not they believe that global revival will one day come, they would surely like to see it. World Evangelism Research Center indicates that *"the country with the fastest Christian expansion ever is China, now at 10,000 new converts every day."* [xvii]

That report was given in 2001, but today, evangelism seems difficult almost everywhere. There are some pockets around the world where folks are still coming to Christ in significant numbers, but these places are few and far between. Individuals, here and there are getting saved, but we are not seeing great revivals. In the nations to which we travel, we see the growth of the church has stagnated and been reduced to a very weak level. The churches we visit seem to be the only bright lights in their area, and they are living in a vast sea of darkness that is covering the nations. The people of these churches are faithful to minister with all that they have, but effective mission work is tough.

Revival is prophesied in the Bible. Revelation 7:9 is only one of several scriptures that speak of an end-time revival, so we know it is coming. Before worldwide revival comes, however, there will be a great falling away. We are experiencing that dark malaise on a global scale. The letters to the seven churches of Asia given in chapters two and three of Revelation, describe the problems of the churches in John's day. These same dynamics are prevalent in the church today. As we approach the hour of the great tribulation, the church will be purged of these errors and then worldwide revival will come. The weakness in the churches of Asia and the modern church (in the Western world) are the same. Here are the main concerns facing the Church as seen in the book of Revelation: Being lukewarm, Fearfulness, Immorality, Tolerating Witchcraft, Casual Faith, and Materialism. Only the Lord can purify His Church and change these dynamics and He will. He will do it before the day of revival arrives. In the meanwhile, we, His people, are exhorted to be faithful to preach and proclaim the good news and to have faith for a harvest. We are to love the Lord and to love people with all of our hearts. We expect good fruit from our labors now and we look, with faith, to the horizon, for the great day of revival that is coming.

World Wide Statistics

Faith and faithfulness are the order of the day for God's people. Rejoice in it and enjoy the journey and try not to beat yourself up or to judge other dynamic Christians for the lack of growth in their churches. It is the spirit of the age we are fighting with, but the Lord will have the final word. he will have His harvest of souls. This book brings a perspective on how that will happen. Let us look at some details regarding the population of the world, Christianity, and missions at this present time.

The population of the world is increasing rapidly. Here are some statistics from July, 2012.

World Population:

- 7,021,836,029
- Median age of people in the world: 28.4 years
- Life expectancy in today's world: 67.07 years [xviii]

Here are some population figures of different countries as of July 2011 according to the CIA World Factbook

Top Ten Most Populous Countries:
(in millions)

- China 1,336.72
- India 1,189.17
- United States 313.23
- Indonesia 245.61
- Brazil 203.43
- Pakistan 187.34
- Bangladesh 158.57
- Nigeria 155.22
- Russia 138.74
- Japan 126.48 [xix]

Among the religions of the world Christianity is the most popular, but that statistic includes all groups who call themselves Christian.

Christians of The World:

Christians:

- 2 Billion worldwide (includes all Catholic, Orthodox, Protestant, etc. joshuaproject.net)
- 6,876 Total People Groups
- 28.6% of the world population

Evangelicals:

- Of the approximate 2 billion Christians in the world today, **648 million (11% of the world's population) are Evangelicals** or Bible believing Christians. Evangelicals have grown from only 3 million in AD 1500, to 648 million worldwide, with 54% being Non-Whites [xx]

United States Missions

"The United States still tops the chart, by far, in terms of total missionaries, sending 127,000 in 2010 compared to the 34,000 sent by No. 2-ranked Brazil.

Also interesting is the fact that South Korea, which previously occupied the No. 2 spot (as detailed in a 2006 CT cover story, "Missions Incredible"), now appears to have been eclipsed by unlikely contenders. According to the CSGC, Brazil, France, Spain, and Italy all sent more missionaries than South Korea did in 2010." (Browse the full results on pp. 76-77 of the report.) [xxi]

Unreached People Groups

While some of these details may look good on paper, the worldwide shortfalls for evangelism are enormous. The number of unreached people groups are staggering and most of the missionary work that is done involves only short term travelling teams. Most of these teams do little to evangelize the world. They usually help encourage local churches and ministries in foreign lands, but most evangelism is done by the local native pastors and the people of their churches.

Unreached People Groups:

- **Total People Groups World-wide:** 16,750
- **Total Unreached People Groups:** 6,921
- **Total Population of Unreached People Groups:** 2.84 billion people
- **Total Percentage of UPG's:** UPG's make up 40.6% of world population [xxii]

American Mission Summary

As Joy and I travel abroad to minister around the world, we are always amazed and blessed to see so many groups of US missionaries travelling on the same flights. Many of them are young people looking to serve the Lord. There is a youthful willingness and a significant effort to send missionaries from the USA to other nations and it does not go unnoticed. Compared to what could be done and what will be done, our US outreach efforts and their effects are tiny. This outreach is grossly insufficient, but it is a consistent trend among young evangelicals.

I am glad to announce that this good trend is only a small indicator of what is to come. The job is not yet being done effectively, but one day the mission movement that flows out of America will become extensive and be extremely successful.

For now, we must do all that we can to spread the gospel. We must also be diligent to pray to the Lord of the Harvest to send forth laborers into the harvest field.

Even in the area of evangelism, the USA is exceptional, not in its scope or effectiveness, but in comparison to what other nations of the world are doing. Her exceptionalism in this regard will be fully demonstrated in the years ahead of us. The Lord Himself, will fulfill this amazing prophecy.

Chapter 14

America's Support For Israel

He Who Blesses Her

The Lord spoke to Abraham and said, "**I will bless those who bless you, and whoever curses you I will curse.**" Gen. 12:3

God has chosen the Jewish people and He has blessed them because of His love for the Patriarchs. Nations that support Israel receive blessings and those who hurt Israel receive curses. One of the ways a nation becomes exceptional, in God's eyes, is when it stands with Israel.

More than any other nation, the USA has (for the most part) sided with Israel and that is one of the reasons why America is exceptional, and why she is blessed. Supporting, defending and blessing Israel is part of the call of God for America; it is part of her end-time purpose.

Early Days

America and the Jewish people have had a connection from the early days of the Republic. President Washington's good friend was a Jewish man named Haym Solomon. His personal money and fund raising skills financed the American Revolution and the founding of the nation.

"On March 25th, 1975, in time for the bicentennial, the United States Post Office issued a commemorative postage stamp which honored him [Haym Solomon] as a Revolutionary War hero. It depicted him seated at a desk. On the front side of the stamp are the words "*Financial Hero*". And, for only the second time in 143 years of U.S. stamps, a message appeared on the back of this stamp, reading:

"Businessman and broker Haym Salomon was responsible for raising most of the money needed to finance the American Revolution and later to save the new nation from collapse." [xxiii]

From the very beginnings, America and the Jews have been connected.

The Modern Moses

A cartoon and article was published in Puck magazine in 1881. It was about Jews coming to America as they fled anti-Semitism and persecution in Europe and Russia. It showed Uncle Sam acting like Moses, parting the Atlantic Ocean and welcoming the Jews to America. The article said,

"All he [Uncle Sam] says to the persecuted races of Europe, whether Jew or Christian, believer or unbeliever, is: "You are welcome to America. Practice any religion you please ... If you wish, cover the land with churches or synagogues ... As my ancient servant predecessor, Moses, did with the Red Sea, I do with the Atlantic Ocean. The waters are divided, and you can safely pass through them to the land of liberty, and leave oppression, persecution and brutality behind you." [xxiv]

From the beginning the presidents of the United States welcomed and encouraged the Jewish people and the founding of the State of Israel. We begin with the words of George Washington.

George Washington

"May the children of the stock of Abraham who dwell in this land continue to merit and enjoy the good will of the other inhabitants; - while everyone shall sit in safety under his own vine and fig tree and there shall be none to make him afraid." [xxv]

The following U.S. Presidents quotes about Jews and their homeland are taken from the Jewish Virtual Library [xxvi]

John Adams (1797-1801)

"I will insist that the Hebrews have done more to civilize man than any other nation." (Letter from John Adams to Thomas Jefferson)

"I really wish the Jews again in Judea an independent nation." (Letter to Mordecai Manuel Noah, 1819)

John Quincy Adams (1825-1829)

[I believe in the] "rebuilding of Judea as an independent nation." (Letter to Major Mordecai Manuel Noah)

Abraham Lincoln (1861-1865)

President Abraham Lincoln met a Canadian Christian Zionist, Henry Wentworth Monk, who expressed hope that Jews ... be emancipated, "by restoring them to their national home in Palestine." Lincoln said this was "a noble dream and one shared by many Americans."

Woodrow Wilson (1913-1921)

"The allied nations with the fullest concurrence of our government and people are agreed that in Palestine shall be laid the foundations of a Jewish Commonwealth." (Reaction to the Balfour Declaration)

"To think that I, the son of the manse, should be able to help restore the Holy Land to its people."

Warren Harding (1921-1923)

"It is impossible for one who has studied at all the services of the Hebrew people to avoid the faith that they will one day be restored to their historic national home."

Calvin Coolidge (1923-1928)

Coolidge expressed "sympathy with the deep and intense longing which finds such fine expression in the Jewish National Homeland in Palestine."

"The Jews themselves, of whom a considerable number were already scattered throughout the colonies, were true to the teaching of their prophets. The Jewish faith is predominantly the faith of liberty."

Herbert Hoover (1928-1932)

"I know the whole world acknowledges the fine spirit shown by the British Government in accepting the mandate of Palestine in order that there might under this protection be established a homeland so long desired by the Jews." (Message for Jewish Organizations Meeting in

Madison Square Garden to Protest the Events in Palestine, August 29, 1929)

"I ... add my expression to the sentiment ... of the Jewish people for the restoration of their national homeland." (Message to the American Palestine Committee, January 11, 1932)

"I wish to express the hope that the ideal of the establishment of the National Jewish Home in Palestine ... will continue to prosper for the good of all the people inhabiting the Holy Land....I have watched ... the rehabilitation of Palestine which, desolate for centuries, is now renewing its youth and vitality through the enthusiasm, hard work and self-sacrifice of the Jewish pioneers who toil there in a spirit of peace and social justice. ... Zionists as well as non-Zionists, have rendered such splendid service to this cause which merits the sympathy and moral encouragement of everyone." (Message to the Zionist Organization of America on the Anniversary of the Balfour Declaration, October 29, 1932)

Franklin Roosevelt (1932-1944)

"The American people, ever zealous in the cause of human freedom, have watched with sympathetic interest the effort of the Jews to renew in Palestine the ties of their ancient homeland and to reestablish Jewish culture in the place ... This year marks the twentieth anniversary of the Balfour Declaration, the keystone of contemporary reconstruction activities in the Jewish homeland. Those two decades have witnessed ... the vitality and vision of the Jewish pioneers in Palestine. It should be a source of pride to Jewish citizens of the United States that they, too, have had a share in this great work." (Greeting to the United Palestine Appeal, February 6, 1937).

"I have on numerous occasions ... expressed my sympathy in the establishment of a National Home for the Jews in Palestine and, despite the set-backs ... I have been heartened by the progress which has been made and by the remarkable accomplishments of the Jewish settlers." (Letter to Senator Tydings, October 19, 1938)

Harry Truman (1944-1952)

"I had faith in Israel before it was established, I have faith in it now." (May 14, 1948)

"This government has been informed that a Jewish state has been proclaimed in Palestine ... The United States recognizes the provisional government as the de facto authority of the new State of Israel." (Granting de-facto recognition to Israel, May 14, 1948)

"I believe it has a glorious future before it - not just another sovereign nation, but as an embodiment of the great ideals of our civilization." (May 26, 1952)

"I am proud of my part in the creation of this new state. Our Government was the first to recognize the State of Israel." (Speech for Conference of the National Jewish Welfare Board, October 17, 1952)

Dwight D. Eisenhower (1952-1960)

"Despite the present, temporary interests that Israel has in common with France and Britain, you ought not to forget that the strength of Israel and her future are bound up with the United States." (Message to Israeli PM David Ben-Gurion, October 31, 1956)

"Our forces saved the remnant of the Jewish people of Europe for a new life and a new hope in the reborn land of Israel. I salute the young state and wish it well."

"The people of Israel, like those of the United States, are imbued with a religious faith and a sense of moral values" (Radio Address on Situation in the Middle East, February 20, 1957)

"The teaching of their ancient belief is filled with truth for the present day. Its profound sense of justice ... is an essential part of every religious and social order. The health of our society depends upon a deep and abiding respect for the basic commandments of the God of Israel." (Statement on Jewish High Holy Days, September 14, 1958)

John Kennedy (1960-1963)

"Let us make it clear that we will never turn our backs on our steadfast friends in Israel, whose adherence to the democratic way must be admired by all friends of freedom." (Speech at Eastern Oregon College of Education, November 9, 1959)

"Israel was not created in order to disappear—Israel will endure and flourish. It is the child of hope and home of the brave. It can neither be broken by adversity nor demoralized by success. It carries the shield of democracy and it honors the sword of freedom." (Speech to Zionists of America Convention, August 26, 1960)

"This nation, from the time of President Woodrow Wilson, has established ... a tradition of friendship with Israel because we are committed to all free societies that seek a path to peace and honor individual right. ... In the prophetic spirit of Zionism all free men today look to a better world and in the experience of Zionism we know that it takes courage and perseverance and dedication to achieve it." (Message to Zionist Organization of America Annual Conference, 1962)

Lyndon Johnson (1963-1968)

"Our society is illuminated by the spiritual insights of the Hebrew prophets. America and Israel have a common love of human freedom and they have a common faith in a democratic way of life ... Most if not all of you have very deep ties with the land and with the people of Israel, as I do, for my Christian faith sprang from yours .... the Bible stories are woven into my childhood memories as the gallant struggle of modern Jews to be free of persecution is also woven into our souls." (Speech before B'nai B'rith)

"I may not worry as much as Prime Minister Eshkol does about Israel, but I worry as deeply." (Conversation with Israeli Ambassador Harman, February 7, 1968)

When Soviet Premier Aleksei Kosygin asked Johnson why the United States supports Israel when there are 80 million Arabs and only three million Israelis, the President replied simply: "Because it is right."

Richard Nixon (1968-1974)

"The United States stands by its friends. Israel is one of its friends. ... The United States is prepared to supply military equipment necessary to support the efforts of friendly governments, like Israel's, to defend the safety of their people." (Speech to the World Zionist Organization)

"Americans admire a people who can scratch a desert and produce a garden. The Israelis have shown qualities that Americans identify with: guts, patriotism, idealism, a passion for freedom. I have seen it. I know. I believe that."

"During the period that I have served as President of the United States, we have been through some difficult times together, and I can only say that the friendship that we have for this nation, the respect and the admiration we have for the people of this nation, their courage, their tenacity, their firmness in the face of very great odds, is one that makes us proud to stand with Israel." (Remarks on Presidential Trip to Israel, June 16, 1974)

Gerald Ford (1974-1976)

"The United States ... has been proud of its association with the State of Israel. We shall continue to stand with Israel. We are committed to Israel's survival and security. The United States for a quarter of a century has had an excellent relationship with the State of Israel. We have cooperated in many, many fields -- in your security, in the well-being of the Middle East, and in leading what we all hope is a lasting peace throughout the world." (Remarks Welcoming PM Rabin to USA, September 10, 1974).

"America must and will pursue friendship with all nations. But, this will never be done at the expense of America's commitment to Israel. A strong Israel is essential to a stable peace in the Middle East. Our commitment to Israel will meet the test of American stead, fairness, and resolve. My administration will not be found wanting. The United States will continue to help Israel provide for her security. My dedication to Israel's future goes beyond its military needs to a far higher priority -- the need for peace. My commitment to the security and future of Israel is based upon basic morality as well as enlightened self-interest. Our role in supporting Israel honors our own heritage."

Jimmy Carter (1976-1980)

"We have a special relationship with Israel. It's absolutely crucial that no one in our country or around the world ever doubt that our number one commitment in the Middle East is to protect the right of Israel to exist, to exist permanently, and to exist in peace." (Presidents News Conference, May 12, 1977)

"I said that I would rather commit suicide than hurt Israel. I think many of them realize the two concepts are not incompatible. If I should ever hurt Israel, which I won't. I think political suicide would automatically result because it is not only our Jewish citizens who have this deep commitment to Israel, but there is an overwhelming support throughout the nation, because there is a common bond of commitment to the same principles of openness and freedom and democracy and strength and courage that ties us together in an irrevocable way." (Speech to the Democratic National Committee, October 22, 1977)

Ronald Reagan (1980-1988)

"Since the rebirth of the State of Israel, there has been an ironclad bond between that democracy and this one ... In Israel, free men and women are every day demonstrating the power of courage and faith. Back in 1948 when Israel was founded, pundits claimed the new country could never survive. Today, no one questions that Israel is a land of stability and democracy in a region of tyranny and unrest ... America has never flinched from its commitment to the State of Israel--a commitment which remains unshakable." (Remarks at National Conference of Christians and Jews, March 23, 1982)

"I welcome this chance to further strengthen the unbreakable ties between the United States and Israel and to assure you of our commitment to Israel's security and well-being. Israel and America may be thousands of miles apart, but we are philosophical neighbors sharing a strong commitment to democracy and the rule of law. What we hold in common are the bonds of trust and friendship, qualities that in our eyes make Israel a great nation. No people have fought longer, struggled harder, or sacrificed more than yours in order to survive, to grow, and to live in freedom" (Remarks at Welcoming Ceremony for PM Menachem Begin, September 9, 1981)

"Israel exists; it has a right to exist in peace behind secure and defensible borders; and it has a right to demand of its neighbors that they recognize those facts. I have personally followed and supported Israel's heroic struggle for survival, ever since the founding of the State of Israel 34 years ago. In the pre-1967 borders, Israel was barely 10 miles wide at its narrowest point. The bulk of Israel's population lived within artillery range of hostile Arab armies. I am not about to ask Israel to live that way again." (Speech on United States Policy for Peace in the Middle East, September 1, 1982)

"The people of Israel and America are historic partners in the global quest for human dignity and freedom. We will always remain at each other's side." (Remarks at Welcoming Ceremony for President Chaim Herzog, November 10, 1987)

George H. W. Bush (1988-1992)

"The friendship, the alliance between the United States and Israel is strong and solid -- built upon a foundation of shared democratic values, of shared history and heritage that sustain the moral life of our two countries. The emotional bond of our peoples goes -- it transcends politics. Our strategic cooperation -- and I renewed today our determination that that go forward -- is a source of mutual security. And the United States' commitment to the security of Israel remains unshakable. We may differ over some policies from time to time ... but never over this principle." (Remarks to Dinner Honoring PM Yitzhak Shamir, April 6, 1989)

" We were with Israel at the beginning, 41 years ago. We are with Israel today. And we will be with Israel in the future. No one should doubt this basic commitment." (White House letter to AIPAC Conference attendees, May 17, 1989)

" Our continuing search for peace in the Middle East begins with it a recognition that the ties uniting our two countries can never be broken ...Zionism is the idea that led to the creation of a home for the Jewish people....And to equate Zionism with the intolerable sin of racism is to twist history and forget the terrible plight of Jews in World War II and indeed throughout history." (Address to the United Nations, September 23, 1991)

Bill Clinton (1992-2000)

"Our relationship would never vary from its allegiance to the shared values, the shared religious heritage, the shared democratic politics which have made the relationship between the United States and Israel a special—even on occasion a wonderful—relationship. ... That unique relationship will endure just as Israel has endured." (Letter to PM Netanyahu on occasion of Israel's 50th birthday)

"America and Israel share a special bond. Our relations are unique among all nations. Like America, Israel is a strong democracy, as a symbol of freedom, and an oasis of liberty, a home to the oppressed and persecuted ... The relationship between our two countries is built on shared understandings and values. Our peoples continue to enjoy the fruits of our excellent economic and cultural cooperation as we prepare to enter the twenty-first century." (Remarks to Israeli Ambassador Shoval, September 10, 1998)

George W. Bush (2000-2008)

"We will ... stand up for our friends in the world. And one of our most important friends is the State of Israel ... Israel is a small country that has lived under threat throughout its existence. At the first meeting of my National Security Council, I told them a top foreign policy priority is the safety and security of Israel. My administration will be steadfast in supporting Israel against terrorism and violence, and in seeking the peace for which all Israelis pray." (Speech to American Jewish Committee, May 3, 2001)

"Through centuries of struggle, Jews across the world have been witnesses not only against the crimes of men, but for faith in God, and God alone. Theirs is a story of defiance in oppression and patience in tribulation — reaching back to the exodus and their exile into the Diaspora. That story continued in the founding of the State of Israel. The story continues in the defense of the State of Israel."(Address on Observance of the National Days of Remembrance, April 19, 2001)

"For more than a generation, the United States and Israel have been steadfast allies. Our nations are bound by our shared values and a strong commitment to freedom. These ties that have made us natural allies will never be broken. Israel and the United States share a common history: We are both nations born of struggle and sacrifice. We are both founded by immigrants escaping religious persecution in other lands. Through the labors and strides of generations, we have both built vibrant democracies, founded in the rule of law and market economies. And we are both countries established with certain basic beliefs: that God watches over the affairs of men and values every human life." (Forward, September 3, 2004)

"Israel is a solid ally of the United States. We will rise to Israel's defense, if need be. So this kind of menacing talk [by the President of Iran] is disturbing. It's not only disturbing to the United States, it's disturbing for other countries in the world, as well.". I made it clear, I'll make it clear again, that we will use military might to protect our ally, Israel." (Speech Regarding War on Terror, March 20, 2006)

"The alliance between our governments is unbreakable, yet the source of our friendship runs deeper than any treaty. It is grounded in the shared spirit of our people, the bonds of the Book, the ties of the soul ... My country's admiration for Israel does not end there. When Americans look at

Israel, we see a pioneer spirit that worked an agricultural miracle and now leads a high-tech revolution. We see world-class universities and a global leader in business and innovation and the arts. We see a resource more valuable than oil or gold: the talent and determination of a free people who refuse to let any obstacle stand in the way of their destiny." (Speech to the Knesset, May 15, 2008)

Barack Obama (2008 - Present)

"The United States was the first country to recognize Israel in 1948, minutes after its declaration of independence, and the deep bonds of friendship between the U.S. and Israel remain as strong and unshakeable as ever." (Statement on the 61st Anniversary of Israel's Independence, April 28, 2009)

"Because we understand the challenges Israel faces, I and my administration have made the security of Israel a priority. It's why we've increased cooperation between our militaries to unprecedented levels. It's why we're making our most advanced technologies available to our Israeli allies. It's why, despite tough fiscal times, we've increased foreign military financing to record levels. And that includes additional support –- beyond regular military aid -– for the Iron Dome anti-rocket system ... So make no mistake, we will maintain Israel's qualitative military edge." (Speech at the 2011 AIPAC Policy Conference, May 22, 2011)

" I think it would be a moral failing for me as president of the United States, and a moral failing for America, and a moral failing for the world, if we did not protect Israel and stand up for its right to exist, because that would negate not just the history of the 20th century, it would negate the history of the past millennium" (Interview with Jeffrey Goldberg in *The Atlantic*, May 21, 2015)

Summary on America's Support of Israel

Many Christians have a love for Israel and an awareness that it is important to stand with and bless the Jewish people.

Many people could easily be disappointed with America during certain seasons when the nation did not stand in support of the Jewish people as much as they could have. Personally, I do not appreciate some of the attitudes or actions by some U.S. Presidents towards the Jews or toward Israel.

It must be noted, however, that to a large degree, America has supported the Jews and Israel with amazing strength and consistency. No other nation has given such incredible support to Israel; like the USA. It has, for the most part, been outstanding and extraordinary.

God blesses and will bless America for her support of the Jewish people. This is one of the dynamics that make America exceptional among the nations.

When global revival covers the earth, it will be Israel and the U.S. leading the way. Pray that we might see the 'One New Man Church', emerge. That will be the family of God, made up of redeemed Jews and Gentiles, preaching the Gospel of Jesus, with love and power. For on the cross, Jesus broke down the middle wall between Jew and Gentile, to make one new man (see Ephesians 2:14-16). The day is coming and America will play a lead role in that revival.

Part 2

Running Away From God

Chapter 15
Jonah Said No

God Sends Jonah

"**The word of the Lord came to Jonah son of Amittai: "Go to the great city of Nineveh and preach against it, because its wickedness has come up before me." But Jonah ran away from the Lord and headed for Tarshish."** Jon. 1:1-2 [Emphasis Mine]

Not Without a Reason

Hindsight reveals that Jonah was the undisputed senior prophet of his day, but we should not think of him as invincible. In fact, his clay feet were clearly exposed when God commanded him to fulfill a task that was out of his league and beyond his gifting. Jonah had, logically speaking, good reason to run from God's directive.

Let's make the case. What if today, a well known, Jewish rabbi was asked to go and preach in Tehran, the capital city of Iran? What if Rabbi Levi Cohan [a fictitious name] was asked to go to the capital city of the enemies of Israel and publically cry out in the streets, *"Repent before the God of Israel, or all of you will die within 40 days"* ?

Would it be a local mob charging with uncontrolled anger, or the national police force, who would be the first to attack him and pull him from his perch? I have witnessed a horrible public stoning in a foreign land and once it begins, I tell you, it is almost impossible to stop.

Anti-Semitism is one of the most hideous expressions of racism and hatred in the world. When I travel to many towns and cities in Europe the Christians tell me, *"You can proclaim any religion on the streets of our city, but if you try to promote Judaism, you will be immediately attacked by a mob of people. People here hate the Jews."*

Recently, while in Poland, I asked my Christian friends for a logical reason for such hatred toward the Jews.

I pointed out:

1.The Jews are not killing people like fanatics of other religious persuasions who advocate suicide bombings, terror and violence in the public square.

2. The Jews are certainly not being religiously overbearing, by trying to evangelize people of other faiths to become proselytes of Judaism. They are not evangelizing, like pushy Mormons or Jehovah Witness groups.

3. The Jews are not dominating the businesses of European cities, in fact, there are so few Jews who still live in Europe. Where once they numbered in the hundreds of thousands, and even in the millions, their numbers have been reduced to a few thousand individuals or less.

4. The Jews are not interfering with government policy. They have no significant place in the politics of the European nations.

So, I asked my friends, "Why such hatred toward the Jews?" After a long pause of silence, they respond, *"It is a good question. We do not know."*

Then inevitably, my friends tell me personal stories of the good relationships that their parents and grandparents had with the Jewish people whom, decades before, lived side by side with them in their communities.

I can only say, *"It must be demonic."* As mentioned in chapter one, from a biblical perspective, the fulfillment of God's promised blessings for Israel and the return of Christ, are linked together. Christ's return means the end of Satan's kingdom, so he does what he can to stop the process. He cannot stop Jesus, so he tries, with all of his might, to stop the Jews. There is a constant demonic frenzy aimed at them. It is the only logical reason for such a maligning of a rather innocent, people group.

The spirit of anti-Semitism is even more aggressive in the Muslim nations. And of those who publically announce death to Jews, Iran leads the charge. Unlike many Europeans, the Islamic nations, do not simply want to silence or ghettoize Jews, they want to wipe them off the map, and kill every one of them.

Jonah's Conclusion

So just imagine if a Jewish rabbi was asked, by God, to go to Tehran to preach the Gospel. We would understand if that rabbi said, *"No God. You have chosen the wrong preacher. Ask a Christian Arab. Please convert one of their own, and let that person preach to his own people. My efforts will be all in vain. They will kill me and my life will be wasted. "*

Wicked Nineveh

In King David's time, it was the Philistines who were the main enemies of Israel. When Jonah was living, it was the Assyrians who were enemy number one to Israel, and their capital city was Nineveh. Today, this is the same people and place as the nation of Iraq, and as previously mentioned, Nineveh is now the city of Mosel.

The reason God send Jonah to Nineveh was to pronounce judgment over them because the city was so wicked (See Jonah 1:2). It was not unfounded fears that Jonah had as he turned his back on Nineveh. This was a warmongering city and her rulers were excessively wicked and barbaric.

We read, **"Assyria (represented by Nineveh, 1:1) had already destroyed Samaria (722-721 B.C.), resulting in the captivity of the northern kingdom of Israel, and posed a present threat to Judah. The Assyrians were brutally cruel, their kings often being depicted as gloating over the gruesome punishments inflicted on conquered peoples. They conducted wars with shocking ferocity, uprooted whole populations as state policy and deported them to other parts of their empire. The leaders of the conquered cities were tortured and horribly mutilated before being executed (see note on 3:3). No wonder the dread of Assyria fell on all her neighbors."** [xxvii]

Stone reliefs, now in the British Museum, show the rulers of Nineveh skinning their captives alive, and dragging prisoners off with metal hooks in their noses.

Tarshish Bound

We can understand why Jonah ran from the Lord. He set sail for Tarshish, which most Bible dictionaries record as most likely being a city in Spain.

Eaton's Bible Dictionary states, **"Where was it? The question as to the locality of Tarshish has given rise to not a little discussion. ... There can be no doubt, however, that this is the name of a Phoenician port in Spain, between the two mouths of the Guadalquivir (the name given to the river by the Arabs, and meaning "the great wady" or water-course). It was founded by a Carthaginian colony, and was the farthest western harbour of Tyrian sailors. It was to this port Jonah's ship was about to sail from Joppa."** [xxviii]

Nineveh was about 500 miles to the east of Jonah's hometown of Gath Hepher, but he was going as far west as he possibly could. The City of Tarshish was on the Iberian Peninsula, more than 2000 miles away, in the opposite direction from Nineveh. It was at the other end of the Mediterranean Sea, in present day Spain. Jonah was determined to separate himself from this mission field as completely and as definitively as possible. Perhaps God would pick someone else, and in return, he would gladly take whatever judgment or penalty that God would give him. Surely, the loss he would receive due to his disobedience could not be worse that trying to preach to the mob in Nineveh.

America is Running

Like Jonah, America is running away from God. The nation is on a downward spiral. The church sees the wickedness of the world and feels unable to do anything about it. Like Jonah, they are deciding to exclude themselves from being a part of the solution.

Regardless, of our churches' influence, our fervent prayers, or our political protests, the United States continues on a course away from its biblical foundations. We are fast leaving the way of the Bible and the Judeo-Christian standard for ethics and morality. I do not blame the church, it is the spirit of the age we are dealing with. We are becoming more and more seeker friendly, but fewer folks are looking in the churches' direction, and many who are seeking, do not want a godly lifestyle change. So many Christians see what is happening and are at a loss to know what to do.

That is why so many Christians have become spiritually disconnected. They believe that God will have to raise up someone else to fix this problem. Perhaps, He will just whisk us all away, in a so-called rapture, and follow through by raining apocalyptic judgment on those who are left behind.

It seems to me that most popular preachers are prophesying judgment on America, but failing to equip the church to be part of God's redemptive plan. I also believe that judgment is coming, but we must not relegate our discussion to judgment alone. I have designated a fourth of this book to the subject of God's judgment. It will come, but I want to focus more on what the church should do about it.

The church has adopted an escapist attitude, but let us quit running from our call. Instead, let's begin to pray, "Lord, Here I am, send me."

Chapter 16

Asleep At The Wheel

Jonah Was Still a Believer

"Jonah had gone below deck, where he lay down and fell into a deep sleep." Jon. 1:5

Jonah was running, but he never stopped being a Jewish prophet and a man of God. When the crew realized that Jonah was the reason for the storm, they spoke with him. **"So they asked him, "Tell us, who is responsible for making all this trouble for us? What do you do? Where do you come from? What is your country? From what people are you? He answered, "I am a Hebrew and I worship the Lord, the God of heaven, who made the sea and the land." Jon. 1:8-9**

Jonah ran from the assignment of preaching in Nineveh, but he never denied the Lord, nor did he renounce his faith. He still proclaimed that he was a Hebrew and that he worshipped the God of heaven. He remained a strong believer, but he had become a rebellious one.

Over the years, I have seen many young people leave the church and wander into the ways of the world. To my surprise, from time to time, they would show up at my door with a non-churched friend. In the process of an earlier conversation they had told their friends that they needed God to help them with their problems. Inevitably they brought their friends to me, and were very glad when I counseled and prayed with them. Although they had left the Christian lifestyle, they never stopped believing and even preaching the gospel to their mates. America is full of those who have forsaken the Lord, but He has not forsaken them and, in the back of their minds, they know the road that leads to life.

American Religious Statistics

According to ABC news, the statistics in the USA show that the vast majority of Americans believe they are Christians. Most do not deny Christ as Savior; they believe in life after death, and they believe they will probably go to heaven after they die. God only knows how true the statistics are or how real the conversions are. Despite the statistics, most Christians in America have definitely forsaken their God assignments, and many have distanced themselves from the Lord and His ways; they are not living a Christian lifestyle. Here are the latest statistics.

"Eighty-three percent of Americans identify themselves as Christians. Most of the rest, 13 percent, have no religion. That leaves just 4 percent as adherents of all non-Christian religions combined — Jews, Muslims, Buddhists and a smattering of individual mentions.

That's quite different from the world at large: Fifty-two percent of the world's population is non-Christian, compared to 4 percent in the United States; and one-third is Christian, compared to 83 percent in the United States. (These are rough comparisons, because the world figures, reported by the Encyclopedia Britannica, are for the full population, while the U.S. figures are among adults only.)" [xxix]

Deep Sleep

I do not believe Jonah was asleep in the bottom of the boat, simply because he was tired. A vicious storm was brewing and he didn't care. He was experiencing inner turmoil and was trying to escape the confusion and the double mindedness that was in his soul. He loved God more than anything, but he was unwilling to obey Him, because His commandment just did not make sense to him. Jonah was soon to discover that he could turn away from Nineveh and even leave Israel, the people and place of his birth, but not leave God. He could go to the farthest end of the known world and physically separate himself 2000 miles from the problem, but he could not hide from God. God was with him in the bow of the boat and God was in the storm.

It seems, the only time Jonah had peace was when he was sleeping, and even then his dreams would haunt him. For a season, it is difficult for a Christian to live in rebellion toward the Lord, but that can change. If a person persists in running away from God, eventually something goes numb and that person will feel dead inside. As people distance themselves from God, their heart becomes an empty place.

It was unbearable so, for Jonah, sleep was his only drug. It was his way to numb the pain and quiet the voice, or the voices in his head. It was not just the Lord who was now speaking; demons and his own flesh were now accusing him and telling him how hopeless and retched he was.

The bottom of the boat was Jonah's way of ignoring reality. It was his attempt to escape the noise in his head and he did not care about the storm above or the problems of other people. Jonah was in an emotion storm and was fighting with all of his might to escape it.

America is Sleeping

Many people in America have said that the White House is asleep at the wheel. There are many home and foreign fronts that have needed a strong resolve but few have been provided.

Foreign armies and terrorists have flourished as America stood by and refused to get involved. As a result, hundreds of thousands of innocent lives have been lost around the world and the security of the U.S. home front is in question. Military ground that had previously been taken has now been lost, and close allies have questioned whether the USA will actually be there when their enemies attack.

Immigration on the home front continues to be a porous and a messy matter. The US administration has not secured her boarders, and unknown factions are infiltrating the land. Drugs, crime, violence and terror are likely growing in the USA because of an insufficiently secured border.

Marriage, the right to life, and personal freedoms have been under attack in recent years and rather than be protected by the government, it has been the White House and the Supreme Court that have caused it. The biblical standard that brought about the American way of life is under attack and its people have been asleep at the wheel.

Our universities, which began as institutions of Christian faith, have by and large, become anti-Christian institutions. Generations of Christian educators have been sleeping as non-Christian instructors have taken over the field. Anti-Christ and anti-God managers have usurped the seats of power in our colleges and resisted Bible-believing professors from entering the halls of instruction. Whole generations are presently receiving a godless education, with a vengeance. The leaders of society are being groomed in these universities to lead America without the Christian God. We have been asleep at the wheel.

The most pervasive instructors within our society are the media. Movies and the TV are determining trends of thought and action for the populous. Entertainment is not innocent. Godlessness is brought into our homes on a daily basis. As a whole, the people and those who should watch over us are asleep while darkness creeps over the land like a thick fog.

Sleeping has Consequences

America has been running away from God. She has been running from her foundations, ignoring her creator, and avoiding her God-given mandate. We cannot blame the government for all of our ills, for those in authority trend toward the consensus of the people. The theology of the masses has shifted and the political parties that connect with them the most get elected. They tend to bring about the wishes of society.

As a pastor, it is easy for me to see how we got this way. I will tell you what I believe to be the root of America's problem and how this present darkness works in our society. Before I do, please understand that I speak in generalities, there are many who refuse to bow their knee to the god of this world. There are many parents who consistently protect their children and guard their homes from vice and godless intrusion. There are also many young people who are totally committed to the Lord Jesus Christ and they will not walk in sin or grovel in the witchcraft of the world. Still, while this godly remnant thrives, many who started well, have chosen to run away from God and America is in trouble because of it.

What is the root of our problem? So many children started well, but were drawn away by the temptations of sin. Rather than repent and obey the Lord, they have rebelled and turned away from Him. Like Jonah, they went to the bottom of the boat, so to speak, trying to ignore God. They indulge in the desires of their flesh and as they do, they push the voice of God further into the background. Soon they become numb and deaf to the Christian message. They become ripe for the enemy's pickings. The devil has come to kill, steal, and destroy, and he wastes no time manipulating people in the pursuit of his goals. The new generation is enticed even more by the godless philosophies of many college professors, and the insidious conspiracies of a sin-saturated media.

Sleeping for a While

Running away and sleeping, rebelling and ignoring God, that was the way of Jonah, and it is the theme of many in our nation. America cannot remain in such a state anymore that Jonah could remain in his deep sleep. There are two reasons why the United States cannot keep this status quo. One is that God has a sovereign purpose and a mission for America to fulfill and He will have the last word and His will is unstoppable. The second reason why America will return to the Lord is because of the prayers of God's people.

There is no nation on earth like the USA that has such a company of saints who battle for a godly government and for righteousness to reign over the land. America has spread the gospel, helped the poor, defended the oppressed and stood with Israel and in so doing, she has claimed the mercies of God. I cannot say how long the dark trend will last or just how dark it will get, but I do know that it will run its course and then the nation will turn to the Lord. That is why we need judgment and why it will surely come.

Chapter 17

America In The Bible

Biblical Prophecy

All of the nations that exist at the end of the age, are mentioned in the Bible, including the United States of America. Furthermore, every nation will experience the judgments of God, and every nation will experience a national revival. The Bible tells us that millions, if not billions, of people from around the world will become disciples of Jesus at one future time in history. They will come from everywhere, from every people group, and every nation on the planet. We read about it in the book of Revelation.

"There before me was a great <u>multitude that no one could count, from every nation</u>, tribe people and language, standing before the throne and in front of the Lamb. They were wearing white robes ... Then one of the elders asked me, "These in white robes- who are they and where did they come from?"... And he said, "These are they who have come out of the great tribulation and have washed their robes and made them white in the blood of the Lamb." Rev. 7:9, 13-14 [Emphasis Mine]

During the great tribulation there will be a revival so enormous that no person can count the number of converts. The Bible says it will happen in every place and that includes America. So the USA, along with all other nations, is mentioned in the Bible. There is much more to learn from the Book of Revelation, so we will devote the next couple of chapters to the apocalyptic message from heaven.

The Book of Revelation

If we want to discover information about the future of the world and the future of America there is no better place to look than the Bible, and more specifically, the book of Revelation.

The first verses of Revelation tell us that this book is the Revelation of Jesus Christ. It is everything about Jesus. It is about His Father, His angels, His church, His earth, His sacrifice, His chosen people, His ministers, His judgments, His revivals, His harvest, and His victory over the devil and over everything that is evil, and much more.

The Book of Revelation shows the fulfillment of the work of the Cross-, for it describes the destruction of Satan's power, and the fulfillment of all of God's blessings that will come to Israel and the church.

There are three series of judgments that are described in great detail; one when the seals are broken off of the scroll, one when the seven trumpets are blown, and one when the bowls of wrath are poured forth.

Between each of these judgments, revival breaks out. Revival is the primary reason for the great tribulation. It is all about the Lord receiving the precious fruit of the earth; men and women who finally yield to become followers of the Lamb (The Lord Jesus).

The great tribulation takes seven years to run its course, because God loves people and He does all that is possible to bring every person into His kingdom. He could simply speak a word and burn the planet to a crisp with unquenchable fire, but He is patient. He could rescue the faithful and destroy the rest, but He patiently gives seven years to the matter of harvesting. Through judgment and pain, people, one by one turn to the Lord.

For thousands of years, God has extended kindness and grace, but people have persisted in their rebellion. At the end of the age, He uses the persuasive power of judgment to wake people up to the truth. These judgments are warranted because of mankind's accumulated sin, but they are not meant to be punitive, they are meant to be redemptive.

Notice what the Bible says about Egypt in the last days. It is an example of what God will do with many nations. **"In that day the Egyptians will be like women. They will shudder with fear at the uplifted hand that the Lord Almighty raises against them. ... The Lord will strike Egypt with a plague; he will strike them and heal them. They will turn to the Lord, and he will respond to their pleas and heal them." Isa. 19:16,22**

As we read the entire chapter of Isaiah 19, we discover the full story of Egypt's future. Before the second coming of Christ, Egypt will become a terrorist nation and will attack Israel as she has done in the past. Israel will defeat Egypt because the Lord will protect the Jewish people. The military power of Egypt and most of her infrastructure will be destroyed until there is almost nothing left and Egypt is writhing in fear and pain. This seems to be a terrible thing, but this will result in a better day for Egypt. Through her pain, Egypt will turn to the Lord and salvation will come to the survivors of that nation. At the end of Isaiah 19, we see Egypt, as a Christian nation, walking hand in hand with Israel and Assyria, who also comes to the Lord.

In Zechariah 14:16-21, we discover that Egypt is a nation that makes it into the millennial reign of Christ. Her temporary suffering and pain caused her to turn around and receive an eternal weight of glory. God resists the proud, but gives grace to the humble. The story of Egypt gives hope to all of the nations of the world.

God's Eye is On America

America is starting from a much better place than Egypt because one's spiritual lineage is very significant. The child of a Christian home, where parents and grandparents, have loved and obeyed the Lord for generations, has a tremendous advantage. Exodus 20, verses 5 and 6, tell us that curses and judgments, due to the sin of witchcraft, can trouble a family for four generations; but it also tells us that God's blessing can extend for a thousand generations for those who love Him.

Many generations of Christians have walked with the Lord in America and God does not forget the ways of the fathers and mothers. Notice what the Lord says concerning Israel, **"As far as election is concerned, they are loved on account of the patriarchs."** Rom. 11:28

God says that He loves Israel because of her patriarchs. Those spiritual parents who walked with God put money in the God bank for their kids. Each generation must choose God for themselves, but God will love them and draw them to Himself if their parents were His friends.

Revival is Certain

Revival is promised to every nation, and if Egypt can turn to the Lord, then without a doubt, America will as well. The question is, 'What will it take for the United States to wake up and become a holy nation? What will it take for America to fulfill her destiny and calling?

In the next chapter we will discover what must change in America so that revival may come. The answer is found in the book of Revelation. Once we see what God is looking for, we can walk in step Him. We can pray, prophesy, teach, preach and watch God fulfill His word according to His sovereign plan and purpose.

Chapter 18

America And The Seven Churches

Keepers of the Book

The Book of Revelation gives us everything we need to have faith for the future. It reveals the problems, exposes the enemy's vulnerability, and declares the undisputable victory of Christ.

Before the details and timeline of the great tribulation are mentioned, Revelation gives us the seven letters to the seven churches of Asia. These churches and their leaders are the keepers of the book. The writings of the Apocalypse had to be kept in a safe place until they could be recorded in our Bibles, so that we would have them two thousand years later.

Each of the churches received an individual copy of the end-time book, each with a dire warning that they were not to add to it, or take away from it (see Revelation 22:18). The author, John, was their spiritual father, the only one of the twelve apostles to be alive, when they received this manuscript.

A Shadow, Not a Code

Each of the seven churches received a personalized letter from God, along with their copy of the great tribulation. In each letter, the Lord told the church about themselves and what they needed to do to improve their disposition.

They were informed of their strengths, their weaknesses and what must be done to make things right. Each was encouraged to be overcomers. If they obeyed the Lord and corrected their sinful ways they were promised amazing rewards. At the end of each letter, a broader word was given, **"He who has ears, let him hear what the Spirit says to the churches." Rev. 3:22**

That final word tells us that the letters were not just for the assigned churches, but for all who would listen. The messages to the churches were also meant for us.

With His predetermined knowledge, in His great wisdom, God knew that these church dynamics would be the same challenges that our generation would have to face. The letter are not given in some secret code, they are a clear foreshadowing of that which was to come. Today, the church around the world is dealing with a mirror image of the same problems that the church had in John's day.

These problems have become a temporary roadblock to the future victory of Christ. They will have to go. The Lord has decided that He will not fulfill His plans without the church being in step with Him. An overcoming church is a requirement for success in the great tribulation.

The Lord Jesus is always many steps ahead of us and we are always working to catch up and get in line with Him. When the time is right, it will not be difficult to assess the church to find out what changes are needed. We can simply study the letters to the seven churches of Asia. They already tell us where we are going wrong and what we have to do.

Uncovering the Weakness

The seven letters are very involved, and exposing every detailed weakness, mentioned in them, would be a great task. It would be most insightful, but for our present purposes, we can draw out the main concerns, and see what major things need to be changed. This can help set us on the correct course. Here is an overview of the overwhelming problems with the church.

1. To the church in Ephesus, we read, **"You have <u>forsaken your first love</u>. Remember the height from which you have fallen! Repent and do the things you did at first." Rev. 2:4-5** [Emphasis Mine]

2. To the church in Smyrna, John wrote, **"<u>Do not be afraid</u> of what you are about to suffer" Rev. 2:10** [Emphasis Mine]

3. To the church in Pergamum, the Lord said, **"You have people there who ... sin by <u>eating food offered to idols and by committing sexual immorality</u>." Rev. 2:14** [Emphasis Mine]

4. To the church in Thyatira, the letter states, **"<u>You tolerate that woman Jezebel</u>, who calls herself a prophetess. ... I will make those who commit adultery with her suffer intensely." Rev. 220-22** [Emphasis Mine]

5. To the church in Sardis, we read, **"<u>You are dead. Wake up!</u> Strengthen what remains and is about to die." Rev. 3:1-2** [Emphasis Mine]

6. To the church in Philadelphia, we receive a different story. **"You have kept my command to endure patiently, I will also keep you." Rev. 3:10**

7. To the church in Laodicea, the scripture says, **"You are neither cold nor hot ... because <u>you are lukewarm</u> ... I am about to spit you out of my

mouth. **You say, 'I am rich ... and do not need a thing. But you ...are wretched, pitiful, poor, blind, and naked. Rev. 3:15-17** [Emphasis Mine]

Roadblocks to Success

When we list the main problems of the ancient church, we discover that they are also the main problems of the modern church. It is easy to discover what needs to be changed. Before America can change, the church in America must change. There are roadblocks hindering God's blessings and victory in the United States, and the first roadblocks to be removed are in the church.

The problems in the church are:

1. A lack of love and passion for Christ.

2. Fear for the future, which means people's trust is not in God.

3. Sexual Immorality, including everything from adultery to deviant perversions.

4. Tolerating witchcraft movies and games in our homes. Allowing religious witchcraft in our churches by not correcting religious manipulation. And allowing sorcery, through false fortune telling that comes from those who minister among us. This is called a spirit of Jezebel.

5. Dead churches who deny the power of the Gospel and resist the work of the Holy Spirit. They have a form of godliness, but deny its power.

6. Materialism has become the god of many people and many churches and God says that is pitiful.

7. Pride and arrogance to think we have everything, when really, many in the church are naked and poor and blind.

Overcomers

Before the church can overcome the devil, she must overcome her own fleshly desires. Since the beginning of time, those fleshly desires include;

1. The lust of the flesh.

2. The lust of the eyes.

3. The boastful pride of life. (See 1 John 2:16).

In the letters to the seven churches, the Lord instructs all of His people to become overcomers. It is expected that they who receive this word will become overcomers. For sure, the end-time church will be a church of overcomers, for it will be a required essential so that the purposes of God may be fulfilled.

Each of the seven churches, except for the church in Laodicea, have at least some who are faithful. Among those churches many actually did amazing exploits for the Lord. That is also true of the church in America today. Many people are outstanding Christians. All of the members of the ancient church could improve and that is true for all of us in the church today. Here is what the Lord told them to do and this is what we must do as well.

1. Repent.

2. Do the godly things you did at first.

3. Be faithful.

4. Renounce darkness, turn around and go in the opposite direction.

5. Hold on to the good that you have.

6. Wake up, and strengthen what remains.

7. Remember what you have seen and heard and obey it.

8. Buy from the Lord gold refined in the fire.

9. Put spiritual salve on your eyes so you can see.

10. Open the door of your heart and let the Holy Spirit come in.

11. Listen to what the Spirit of God says to the churches.

12. Be overcomers, both of the flesh and of the devil.

Keys Gathering Dust

The Lord has shown the church what keys will open the prison doors and allow success to come to His people and to the nation. He gave keys to the early disciples so that they could bind and loose demonic powers to set the captives free (see Matthew 16:19).

Jesus is still distributing keys of authority today, but before we can unlock the works of darkness over the nation, the works of darkness must be removed from the church.

It is one thing to diagnose a problem, but something else to see the remedy unfold. How will positive change come and when will it happen?

The Lord is patient and merciful, but the church continues to sleep in the bow of the proverbial boat while the nation is running away from God. Most of her people, from the highest courts in the land to the first year students of our colleges are ignoring the Word of the Lord.

The only possible road to redemption is judgment and suffering. If there was another way, I believe God would utilize it. As with Jonah, while he slept in the bow of the boat, judgment is fast approaching the United States.

The keys of authority are gathering dust. They wait for a people and a time when their powers will be ignited and the purpose will be seen. That day will be the church's finest hour.

Chapter 19

Disqualified Leaders

Wounded Warriors

Another reason for the sleeping church in America is the disqualification of so many spiritual leaders. If Satan can sideline his most powerful adversaries, he will have accomplished his goal. The land is full of mature saints who have become wounded warriors. Many have chosen a form of spiritual sleep as an escape from their pain.

So many church veterans have stepped into the shadows of inactivity because they were victimized, hurt, or have become disillusioned with the church. They still believe in God, but no longer connect with His people in a dynamic way; they have backed up and withdrawn. They have stepped away from their leadership roles because of a number of reasons. These include sexual and moral failure, abusive church politics, selfish ambitions, unfulfilled expectations, and / or, various personal attacks against their marriages, their children, their financial stability, or their health.

Satan uses any and all tactics to disqualify those people who could harm him the most, and at this present time, the casualty count among church leaders is extremely high. Christians talk about spiritual warfare coming against prayer meetings, Sunday services, and showing up in national politics. That is a real concern, but they may fail to see that the greatest attacks of spiritual warfare are much closer to home. They are personal attacks against individual Christians, especially church workers, leaders and their families.

Failure of Pastors

Although most leaders of God's church do not fall into sin, some do. Pastors, their wives, and other senior leaders within the church, live in the same immoral society as everyone else. They can be affected by its sinful influence and temptations, like any other person. Paul warns leaders to guard their souls against the pressures of temptation, lest while they have preached to others, they themselves should become castaways (see 1 Corinthians 9:27, Romans 2:21).

When church leaders, at any level, fall into sin, the effects are far reaching. Churches lose their momentum, and some of them take such a beating, usually from their own people, that they cease to exist. The leader in question is almost always disqualified from the ministry, even after he changes his ways. It is extremely rare that he or she can ever return to the same level of ministry as before.

All of the leaders who where disciples of that senior fallen leader will also become dysfunctional, because of dissolution or ministry collapse.

Sin is difficult to deal with and the church has not found a graceful way of reinstating her fallen generals. People can forgive but it is very hard to regain trust and confidence once it has eroded. The sad story reveals wounded people, broken homes, devastated churches, and disqualified leaders.

Selfish Ambition

Idealistic Christians are great; people should hold to a high level of expectant kingdom power and blessings. They should always believe in them, and have the faith to see them unfold before their eyes. Often, there is a mixture, however, of godly calling, opportunism, and even selfish ambition.

I heard the late Derek Prince say, "The greatest problem in the church today is selfish ambition."

Sometimes the expectations that people have are wrapped up in their own aggrandizements. It is personal pride and attention that pushes them on to serve in the church. The truth is they are only happy when they are being promoted. If they are not promoted they will grieve and they may even be destructive.

There is an old adage, "If a person complains when they are left out, they will be puffed up when they are brought in."

I do not know who first said it, but it is often true. The sad thing is that many of these ambitious folk have tremendous gifting, but they have a blind spot when it comes to self-evaluation. If only their character matched their talents they would be great workers and leaders in God's house. As it is, because of their pride, many are not given positions of leadership, and others simply abandon ship because they feel extremely unappreciated.

Unfulfilled Expectations

Some who are not prideful are also overlooked even though they have amazing gifting. This may be because the church is too small and there is simply not enough meetings or people to warrant more leaders. There is no room for them in their present church environment.

Other times, the senior pastor is a cork in the top of the bottle. He has a one-man show. He does all of the worship leading, all of the preaching, all of the small group teaching, all of the pastoral visitations, and all of the church administrative, decision-making. After a while, people stop serving because their gifting is not being utilized. They are called to leadership but the senior pastor will not let them lead.

This is an indictment against the church for it takes the whole body of Christ to do the whole will of God. It is an insecure pastor who does not share the workload with other members of Christ's body. When this happens the devil becomes the winner and the leaders who could be serving tend to drift off into a deep spiritual sleep.

Church Politics

Politics is not really a bad word, it simply means to organize, manage and lead people. As such, we could have good or bad politics. It just depends on the management and the leadership of the politicians.

Churches are communities of people so there will always be some politics, we just trust that it is good politics. All too often, policies, prejudices, and priorities, displace the important dynamics of love and care of people.

Folks feel like they are being used, or that they are being pushed around, patronized, and overlooked. Soon they feel unimportant as if they are just numbers and not people.

It can even get much worse; some leaders actually attack their own sheep. They may degrade them or correct them so harshly that they inflict serious wounds. This is the worst kind of insecurity. Some folks seem to think that putting down the skills or character of others will lift them to a superior position. The opposite is true, whenever you put someone else down, you hurt yourself and the way people see you.

When that abuse is then shared in critical gossip with other members of a church, it becomes unbearable and drives people away from that church. We call this, "Church Politics," and it is all too common in church life.

This has a lasting negative effect on the leaders who were shoved out of the church. It means they will hesitate before serving in the next church they attend and if it happens a few different times in several different churches, they will be ruined for life. Again, the devil is the only winner of that outcome.

Most of those dislodged leaders hold their tongues. They have no interest in spreading ill remarks about the church or the pastors they have left. That is an honorable resolve, but with it they often become absolutely quiet. They do not enter into heartfelt fellowship with other believers or even share the Gospel with sinners. They are wounded and they go into a spiritual slumber. They focus on loving their families and helping a few friends here and there, but their global kingdom mandate has been lost. Only the devil is rejoicing with this result.

Personal Attacks

The devil is a roaring lion, roaming the earth, seeking whom he can devour. He takes the innocent and the vulnerable, but his big prize is the leaders of God's church and kingdom. When he removes a leader from serving, he wipes out their work and the people who they would have helped.

His personal attacks against the workers of Christ are obvious. This weekend, as I write, my daughter Elizabeth and son-in-law, Jesse have left to lead an outreach mission in New York. They will be helping a new church plant in a poor neighborhood where there is a great need. I will bring the rest of the church team and join them in a couple of days. Wouldn't you know it, a water pipe in their house burst last night. You might say, that is a bad coincidence with really bad timing. This incident is not due to their negligence. The pipe did not freeze, they live in South Carolina. It was a manufacturer's defect in the water pipe. The fact that it burst just before the trip, when they are absolutely inundated with all of the work and details of the mission, is more than suspicious. It is a demonic conspiracy against them. The devil comes to wear out the saints of the Most High God, especially when they are attacking his kingdom of darkness.

For decades, I have watched as the devil hurled attack after attack against my wife and me just before we were heading toward a major mission or a significant church event. It never stopped us, and as a result, I am sure we are attacked less now then in the early days of our ministry. It is as if, he has learned that it is futile to hassle us, because we are determined to press on. His attacks actually make us more aggressive so he has learned to back off. But, I see, he goes after the younger crowd all the time.

I have watched so many start a great ministry but come under intense attack and pull back. National leaders have passed the baton to others before their term was over and the result was a weakening of the mission. The devil's attacks come in the form of sickness, financial stress, strife in the family and perhaps the hardest one to handle, severe sickness affecting your children.

Some leaders have actually been killed in accidents or through such hideous diseases as cancer, or a heart attack. We are in the middle of a massive war and there are too many officers who are falling prey to the enemy. Many are simply backing off, refusing to fight any longer. Many leaders are now lying on the hammock, in the yard, sleeping while the storm of the ages is brewing.

The weapons of our warfare are not carnal, but mighty through God to the pulling down of strongholds (see 1Corinthians 10:3). Be strong men and women of God. Take your stand, walk in holiness, rise up and win the day.

Wake up ye servants of the most high God, the day of His victory is approaching fast. He will give you strength and the people of God will volunteer freely in the day of His power (see Psalm 110:3).

Chapter 20

Wake Up Jonah

The Captain's Call

"The captain went to him and said, "How can you sleep? Get up and call on your god! Maybe he will take notice of us, and we will not perish." Jon. 1:6

Inevitably, judgment will strike the entire globe because of man's accumulated crimes against humanity and the creator. Curses are already hanging over the human race, and the book of Revelation describes the judgments that will fall on the nations because of unrepentant sins.

It is not God who planned the sin of the world, but He does initiate the judgments that follow, for such sin cannot be left unanswered. Two thousand years ago, He instructed John to record the details of these coming judgments and to send them to the seven churches of Asia. In His foreknowledge, God knew the path of destruction that will come, even though He desires and asks for the opposite. His sovereignty does not overstep the will of man, and in the end, He knows what man will do and what judgments must follow.

The intensity of these judgments, however, may be different for every nation. It will be determined by a nation's righteous, or sinful acts. Righteousness exalts a nation, but sin is a reproach to any people (see Proverbs 14:34). The nations will not suffer equally during the great tribulation. For example, Israel will experience special favor during much of great tribulation. She will experience supernatural, military protection, as God Himself, shields and defends her (see Zechariah 12). She will also experience a national revival during the early days of the great tribulation (see Zechariah 13:1-2).

The special favor comes because Israel has a predetermined calling and mission from God, but I think, the United States has a predetermined calling and mission as well. Besides their God-ordained mission, these nations have an added advantage because of the prayers and lives of their ancestors. Notice what the Lord says concerning Israel, **"As far as election is concerned, they are loved on account of the patriarchs,** [their ancestors] **for God's gifts and his call are irrevocable." Rom. 11:28-29**

What About America

As I see it, the issue is, can our leaders wake up and change the present course of America? My first request is not directed toward America's political leaders, but her church leaders. Even here, I am not primarily referring to the pastors, for they are a small minority of the total church leadership. Like with the captain on Jonah's ship, the Lord is our captain, and He is calling the vast multitude of unrecognized leaders to wake up in America.

God's perspective is not the same as man's perspective. The church may identify a clergy/laity separation, but God has leaders in both groups and the number of those who are not recognized as clergy greatly outnumber the recognized leaders of the clergy.

There is a sleeping giant in the church. It is a vast army of men and women who have received spiritual authority and gifting from heaven. The Lord desires a dynamic move of His Holy Spirit power through these leaders and into the world. Similar to the sending forth of His first disciples, Jesus desires to send a multitude of new disciples to the nations. He says, **"The harvest is plentiful, but the workers are few. Ask the Lord of the harvest, therefore, to send out workers into the harvest field. Go! I am sending you as lambs among wolves." Lk. 10:2-3**

The outcome of nations and specifically, the nation of America, will be determined by the behavior of these leaders. We can start the process in prayer as we fervently ask the Lord to wake up His church and send workers into the harvest field.

If My People

Can we hear the captain's call?

King Solomon built the first temple as instructed by the Lord. When it was finished, he prayed and asked God if He would hear the prayers of the people if they were lifted up to Him from this temple. The response was amazing.

The Bible says, **"When Solomon had finished the temple ... the Lord appeared to him at night and said: "I have heard your prayer and have chosen this place for myself ... When I shut up the heavens so that there is no rain, or command the locusts to devour the land or send a plague among my people, <u>if my people, who are called by my name will humble themselves and pray and seek my face and turn from their wicked ways, then I will hear from heaven and will forgive their sins and heal their land.</u>" 2 Chr. 7:11-14** [Emphasis Mine]

The Lord is saying that He may send locusts, drought and plagues, as judgments against His people because of their sin. He also gives a remedy that will alleviate those judgments. He tells Israel that the judgments can be lifted if the nation stops its evil behavior. Curses can be broken and judgments can be avoided if the people will do four things. They must humble themselves, pray, repent, and turn from their wickedness. In response to those changes, God promises three powerful blessings. He says He will hear from heaven, forgive the people of their sins, and then He will heal their nation.

Revival and The Great Tribulation

This process of national healing will actually happen to Israel sometime during the first two years of the great tribulation. We will talk about this in greater detail later in the book.

For now, we need a right perspective on the great tribulation. We need to understand that the Book of Revelation is more about redemption and blessings, than it is about judgment and trauma. The pain and chaos is an essential means to an end. The violence and judgments of the tribulation will be extremely severe, but this is the only way to save mankind from lasting destruction and eternal damnation. The judgments of Revelation are justified, but the final outcome shows that mercy overcomes judgment. Where sin abounds, God's grace does much more abound. The book of Revelation presents an amazing picture of God's abundant mercy and grace. It can be seen, not just at the end of the book, but all the way through it. If the world could only shift and embrace the four prescribed steps of humility, (humility, prayer, repentance, and godly change) before the great tribulation begins, it could remove the global curse and lift the devastating judgments before they fall. The judgments could be avoided, but God knows that the world, as a whole, will not repent without the judgments falling, so the great tribulation is unavoidable.

Nineveh Did It

A ruinous judgment was prophesied over Nineveh, but as we will discover, the entire city repented and for a season, the curse was lifted. God gives adequate opportunity for man to turn away from evil. Some may think that He is too patient in this matter, and wish that He would punish wickedness sooner, rather than later, but the Lord is compassionate and slow to anger. No human has ever, or will ever be judged by God prematurely, or inappropriately.

If Nineveh, the wicked city of violence and abuse, can make the shift to turn from her wicked ways, then cannot other cities and nations do the same? And if they do, will not the God of all grace lift His judgments from them as well?

Sleeping Saints

The outcome of America's eminent future lay in the hands of her broad-based church leadership. As goes the leaders of the church, so goes the church, and as goes the church, so goes the nation. America is still a nation of strong believers, and all things are possible to them that believe. The problem is that the majority of American church leaders are snoozing.

The American Sleep Association says there are five different stages of sleep. To start with, there is light sleep, but as sleep continues it gets more intense until it reaches a really deep sleep. During the lightest stages of sleep, people may not even realize they have been sleeping, if they wake, because the mind is still semi-conscious of its surroundings. In the heaviest stages of sleep, it may be difficult to wake some people up. It can be almost like a state of coma. People typically move through the five stages of sleep several times during one night.

It takes between one and two hours for a sleep cycle to be completed. It starts very light and moves progressively toward deep sleep, then returns to start the cycle over again. I think that the multitudes of church leaders who have been distracted, or severely wounded, have chosen spiritual sleep as an escape. They are presently in different levels of the sleep cycle. Perhaps some can be woken, but others cannot be stirred because of the deep sleep stage they are in.

Only God can wake the sleepers. Perhaps, God will send a relatively light series of judgments over America to start with. Perhaps this will stir the sleeping giant and the church will arise. Let us pray for God's mercy. Let us pray that those judgments will not have to be too severe.

Chapter 21

Can The White House Wake Up?

The Choice is Ours

It is not only America's church leaders who are snoring, our political leaders are also asleep at the wheel. We need a shift in the White House, but our leaders are elected officials. They are only a reflection of the attitudes and moral beliefs of the majority of Americans. Politicians walk on the road where society runs. They tend to flesh-out the spiritual climate of the nation. If the populous is godly, the politicians will rise toward that position. If the majority of the people are corrupt, their leaders will be as well. Even when a segment of the nation is righteous, in a democracy, the government leaders will still follow the majority.

There are potential blessings in the politics of America. The blessed thing is that the hearts of the populous can change, and if they do her leaders will change. With the right motivation people can reverse the trend of secular humanism and return to the absolutes of the Bible.

God Initiates Political Change

I am always amazed at the creative methods and the surprising changes that God initiates to release His mercy and grace over nations. I know it is always in partnership with the prayers of His people.

Russia

Although it did not bring revival, there was good political change over Russia. The people of the Soviet Union were in a political prison, and no one expected the "Iron Curtain" to come down when it did in 1989.

I, along with the whole world was shocked, but blessed, when President Mikhail Gorbachev announced the removal of the Berlin Wall. It fell on November 9, 1989 and celebration erupted around the globe. One year earlier, the President of the United States, Ronald Reagan, gave his famous speech asking for this resolve. On June 12, 1987, he spoke with power and authority and said, **"Mr. Gorbachev, tear down this wall!"**

I believe that God moved both of these men to say and do what was necessary. Before it happened, most people expected the Iron Curtain to remain far into the foreseeable future, but God had a different plan. When people pray, He moves in the political affairs of the nations.

Israel

The political events that led to the establishment of the restored State of Israel in 1948 are modern day miracles. One hundred years before her birth, the idea of Israel becoming a nation was scorned and laughed at. It was seen by the entire world, including the Catholic and Protestant Church, as a ridiculous idea. It was seen as totally impossible and completely unnecessary.

The political resistance toward nationhood, from within the Jewish community, and from the Gentile world, was enormous. Only a relatively small group of people prayed and believed for the rebirth of Israel. Then, in fulfillment of forty-seven different biblical prophecies, Israel was born.

It came about through enormous pain and suffering, that found its worst days of terror in the Nazi Holocaust. Before that time, even though the Jewish people had been horribly abused and persecuted for hundreds of years, most of them were not willing to leave the lands of the Gentiles to start a new nation in the Holy Land.

After the Second World War, both Jews and many Gentiles agreed that the chosen people should have their own nation. God raised up the political will among the nations for an international consensus toward this purpose. On November 29, 1947, the United Nations voted in favor of the establishment of a Jewish state and the word of God was fulfilled.

Even more phenomenal was the providence of God in 1948 to help and protect the young nation survive as she was attacked from every side by the Arab nations around her. For six months, Israel was attacked and singlehandedly defended her land, and her people. Many miraculous signs and wonders were reported until, in January of 1949, her War of Independence subsided.

Israel has fought for her right to exist since that day, and God has watched over her consistently. The USA partnered with her starting in the 50's, and once again, we conclude, that God is at work in the political affairs of the nations.

England

Miraculous stories are told throughout history of special times when God intervened as people prayed. Such a moment occurred on July 29, 1588 when the Catholic Spanish Armada was crossing the English Channel to attack and overtake Protestant England.

Queen Elizabeth 1, who was later hailed as the English Deborah (after her biblical counterpart) defeated the Spanish army by an act of God. She and her people prayed and God protected them from certain destruction.

At that time, Spain was the most powerful country in the world. Only tiny England and the Dutch Republic stood in the way of Spain's domination over Europe. England was poor and possessed no overseas lands or colonies at that time.

The plan of the Spaniards was to invade England, remove Elizabeth and put Isabella on the throne. Then they would force England to become Catholic, and Spain would rule the world.

Worse than it might seem, **"The ships were filled with fanatical Jesuits ... and their racks and pulleys, thumbscrews, iron virgins, gridirons and other diabolical instruments of torture to be used once the Spanish inquisition was set up in England."** [xxx]

The Spanish had over one hundred and thirty war ships heading for the coast of England. To add to their strength, armies from the Netherlands and Portugal had also set sail to join them in the attack. The Spanish Armada and their allies seemed invincible.

It was believed that they would totally overwhelm England but, standing in faith before God, Queen Elizabeth would not surrender. As the battle began, Queen Elizabeth, to live or die, entered the fight with her troops, mounted on a white horse.

Suddenly, a violent storm, sent by God, arose on the sea. The Spanish ships were on fire by a counter attack from the smaller and outnumbered British ships. Then they were blown off course by an act of God, and most of them were destroyed in the storm. The majority of Spanish soldiers were lost at sea, and never returned home.

A bronze plaque was erected at St. Paul's Cathedral after a national service of thanksgiving to God. It read, **"God blew and they were scattered."**

The Battle Against Slavery

One of the greatest stains in the history of America, is slavery. As I write this book, the confederate flag is being removed from the state properties of South Carolina, where I live. The flag represents a political system that embraced and encouraged slavery, even after it was opposed by the rest of the nation, therefore its removal is long overdue. What a horrible thing slavery is, and what misguided behavior would celebrate any history that fought to keep it?

President Abraham Lincoln, championed the cause to legally remove slavery from America, nevertheless, we are still fighting the battle for equality today. He fought long and hard to bring an end to this horrific injustice, and he often mentioned his need and dependence on God, as the battle for freedom raged on.

As president of the United States, Lincoln stood for the principle, that all men are created equal under God. He stood for righteousness, and he literally gave up his life, because he wanted godliness in America. The Civil War was too long and too gruesome, but it was a necessary, because those who insisted on slavery would not relent. Lincoln would not give up either, and he was sure that in the end, God and right would prevail.

He wrote, **"Amid the greatest difficulties of my administration, when I could not see any other resort, I would place my whole reliance on God, knowing that all would go well, and that He would decide for the right"**
xxxi

It Will Happen Again

There is no doubt, that even today, Abraham Lincoln is revered as the greatest US president of all time. During his presidency, and during many other presidential terms of office, a man of God was in the White House. It will definitely happen again.

God will surprise us because in His own way and at the right time, He will raise up a leader who will champion the cause of godliness for America once again.

As He has answered the prayers of His people in so many nations throughout history, He will do it for America in answer to the prayers of her people.

Yes, the White House can wake up, but we must first see the political will of the people, and we must first see the spiritual will of church leaders woken up.

It will come, but what necessary trauma must we face this time, before the nation will turn from its running and wake from its slumber. God only knows.

Part 3

Judgment Over America

Chapter 22

Dark Clouds Coming

Critical Mass

This terrified them and they asked, "What have you done? (They knew he was running away from God because he already told them so)." Jon. 1:10

The cargo ship was out at sea, and on its way to Tarshish. Jonah was in a deep sleep in the bow of the boat, and why not, the sailors were veterans of the waves; the crew was hearty and sea worthy.

Jonah was in a spiritual sleep, he was denying the voice within him, and running away from God. He was tied to the wrong course, bound in his mind, and set in his ways. He had no desire for God's assignment, and nothing but death itself could change his mind and turn him around.

Jonah's rebellious behavior was the sole reason why God sent the death storm. It was not a warning, those days were past; this was a reckoning, it was judgment day. Jonah was willfully fighting God and he was about to lose the fight.

I am sure that the Lord had given Jonah an extensive array of spiritual information so that he could not say he did not know. He had probably given him dreams, visions, signs from heaven, and maybe even an angelic visitation, or He had spoken to him directly in an audible voice. The word of the Lord was clear and no doubt, it was repeated, but Jonah did everything he could to ignore it. First he recognized it, then he refuted it, and finally, he rejected it. Jonah had his back up, and he would not be moved. Stubbornness is as the sin of witchcraft and Jonah's stubbornness had turned into rebellion. It had become an angry refusal within him, and he was leaning toward a seared conscience.

There is a time to wrestle with the Lord, and there is a time when God will allow wanderings, willfulness and even wickedness.

There is also a time, when the Lord refuses to let a situation lie. Perhaps it is because of prayer. Certainly, it is because He initiates action for the unfolding of His universal plan. That is never negotiable. That will always move forward regardless of the lack of cooperation from mankind.

There is also a time when the cup of sin is full, and the cry of the innocent reaches critical mass. Then in His wisdom, God says, "enough is enough," and nothing can stop or even slow down, His will or purpose.

From Fear to Faith

Despite the skill of the mariners, the storm they faced was beyond any ability or expertise they might muster. They could not get to shore, and the hardened sailors soon feared for their lives.

This was the same body of water that the Apostle Paul was sailing on, when a devastating storm engulfed his Roman war vessel. On that occasion, the craft was violently tossed for fifteen days and nights. The wind was roaring, the lightning cracking, and the rain was a constant blinding deluge. As with Jonah's ship, they threw everything overboard, but it was to no avail.

Finally the Roman galley was ripped to pieces, and 276 souls were fighting for their lives in the boisterous billows of the shark-infested Mediterranean Sea. There are forty-three different varieties of sharks in the Mediterranean.

Paul had been visited by an angel the night before. He told the people that all they possessed, along with the ship, would be lost, but they would survive. As the main body of the ship sunk to the depths of the sea, the people clung to pieces of broken debris.

They were washed ashore and instantly cared for by the natives of that place. God had demonstrated that the Roman fleet was not in charge. He had a sovereign purpose for His servant, Paul, and He set the stage for a paradigm shift. He used the storm to elevate Paul to a new level of respect. This opened the hearts of the sailors and of many Romans who would hear the story in the days and months to come.

Even the natives were given a demonstration of God's power when they saw a poisonous snake fall from Paul's hand into the fire. Many people came to the Lord on the island and later in Rome, because of the testimony of Paul's triumph over the storm. God has His ways of turning impossible situations around. Sometimes, His greatest demonstrations involve near-death events. When only a miracle will save people, a miracle is given, and it is exactly what is needed to turn the hearts of people to the Lord.

America, a Storm is Brewing

A storm is brewing over America. Since September 11, 2001, when a group of Muslim terrorist flew a commercial jetliner into the World Trade Center in New York City, the country has been on high alert.

Hundreds of Christian authors have warned the nation, through thousands of books and articles, of the impending doom of God's judgment that is coming. Thousands of pastors and teachers have preached sermons of heaven's justice that will soon fall on America because of her sins. The message has been carried on the airwaves, through various Christian radio and TV programs. They may choose to ignore it, but the Church has heard the warnings.

It is not just the Church that knows of impending doom; the whole country embraces this fear. The entire nation is focused on the possibility of immense carnage coming to our country.

News broadcasters tell story after story, of relatively small, yet still horrible, and deadly, terrorist attacks that frequent our streets since 9/11. And beyond that, they continuously highlight many threats against the security of America that have been averted by the U.S. intelligence agency.

Starting with George W. Bush, the word I have often heard repeated by representatives of the White House is, **"To bring disaster, the terrorist only need to be successful once, but to stop disaster, we need to be successful one hundred percent of the time."**

Government officials confess that it is impossible to detect and catch every enemy, all the time. Fear is brooding over the people of America, and that fear is not going away. There is an underlying suspicion that things will only get worse; that our enemies are becoming more emboldened, and more devious in their conspiracies against us. It is only a matter of time until calamity will strike. We will have to deal with it when it comes, but the fact that it is coming, is certain and unavoidable. From day to day, the people get on with their lives, but the fear threshold is close at hand. Fear lurks just below the waves and readily shoots to the surface, every time a new violent incidence occurs.

The Skill of the Sailors

In Jonah and Paul's day, the masterful skill of the sailors could not save them. Even the non-Christian crew was not naïve, they had a strong respect for the sea and a strong fear of the gods. The fear of the Lord, the God of Israel, was all they needed, but at the beginning of their stories, they did not know Him.

I am thankful for the skill of the CIA, the FBI and other departments of the U.S. government that devote their energies toward the security of America. I believe with their talents and the prayers of God's people, many attacks have been thwarted or diverted.

When God's judgment comes, however, there will be no stopping it. They can throw everything overboard, pull out all the stops, reign in all of their experts, and use the most amazing technical devices, but it will not help. Only prayer, repentance, and a shift in behavior with stay the hand of God.

The storm may, simultaneously, come from many directions. It may include excessive natural disasters, civil unrest and riots, deadly plagues and viruses, and terrorist attacks.

If all of these things conspire against us at the same time, it would not take long to deplete our finances and bankrupt the nation.

Pray for God's mercy, a massive storm is coming and our government cannot the people.

Chapter 23

What Have We Done?

Who is Guilty?

"What have you done? (They knew he was running away from God because he already told them so)." Jon. 1:10

The captain asked, "Jonah, what have you done?" Today, as we talk about judgment coming, we ask, "America, what have you done?"

When I compare the evil I see in America with what I have seen in other nations, I must admit the USA does not come across as being the worse sinner in the world.

Human rights violations are much worse in many countries around the globe. I have a difficult time thinking about it too much, and there are some popular historical war movies that I find difficult to watch. I can't get my head around it. I find it hard to fathom the torture, the mass murders, and the violent abuse of women and children that have been perpetuated by various regimes, around the world, in recent years, and even to this present day.

Certainly, over the past one hundred years, the barbarism of the Nazis, the Communists, and different ethnic peoples and tribes, against their neighbors, has been beyond the pale.

Perhaps, because my mother's birth name was Katz, and my research revealed that more than seven thousand people with that last name were murdered in the Nazi death camps, that torture and abuse seems very close to home. The amount of innocent blood that has been shed, and the number of lives that have been taken, because of power-hungry, greedy, bigoted men, is enormous.

Today, we are still seeing the beheadings of innocent people by Muslim fanatics such as ISIS and the Taliban. These things, however, are not new, they have been happening since man has ruled over man, and many nations that we now call respectable were, in generations past, guilty of these same crimes.

I do not think we need to go into the details of various torture methods, or discuss the details of the huge volume of recorded war crimes to validate the fact that evil exists in the heart of men. Apart from God, mankind will revert to barbarism.

The so-called Christian Church has been just as guilty as the non-religious dictators. Hundreds of years ago, murder and genocide were perpetuated throughout the civilized world, in the name of the Christian God, and with so-called Christian motives.

The Spanish Inquisition is just one time period in history where people tortured people, in the name of Christ. They did it, supposedly, to purify the Christian Church. The barbarism of the Jesuit priests involved, was as wicked and demonic, as anything I have researched from any other expression of witchcraft, in any country, throughout all of man's history. We called the native people who sacrificed European explorers and settlers, barbaric savages, and so they were. The Church, however, during the Inquisition was, every bit, just as savage.

Only God can judge if these people were really Christians. Personally, I have a difficult time believing it. Just because someone calls themselves a Christian does not mean they have a ticket to heaven. God judges a man or woman on their behavior as well as their faith in the cross of Christ. In fact many will come to God on the Day of Judgment saying, "We called out in your name, Lord, Lord! We gave ourselves to many religious exercises." But He will say to them , "Depart from me into outer darkness, you workers of iniquity, I never knew you" (see Matthew 7:22-14).

If people are workers of iniquity, Jesus will cast them into Hell, no matter how well they know the Bible or how great a number of people are following them.

Perhaps the further back in history, the easier it is to distance ourselves from the horrors of government sponsored evil. When we think of it happening in our lifetime, or in the lifetime of our parents, it is hard to imagine. Maybe because we have the idea that educated men do not commit such atrocities. Maybe we think, if only we can be better educated, then evil will be confronted and it will stop.

That has not proven to be true. The civilized, educated men of the twentieth century were just as vile as their less educated ancestors. It seems that educated men, apart from God, are just a smarter criminals.

Education alone does not change a person's heart. He may simply extend the carnage to more people, and do it more efficiently, or with more deviant methods. When visiting the Nazi concentration camp, 'Dachau', in Munich, Germany, I saw what educated men could do. I saw the photos and read about the scientific experiments perpetrated by educated doctors and scientist there. They devised sophisticated contraptions and operations to torture innocent people to their death. They did this simply to discover the amount of pain and abuse a human being might be able to suffer before dying.

We live in a more educated world, but look how many people were killed because of war, over the past one hundred years. Here are estimated totals for the one hundred years between the years 1900 and 2000. The number of people who died in all the wars, massacres, slaughters and oppressions during the Twentieth Century is a staggering 258,327,000 (Two hundred and fifty eight million, three hundred and twenty seven thousand). [xxxii]

Greed, racism, power mongering, racial pride, and religious bigotry, drive people to malicious violence as much today as it ever has been.

Slaves in America

Slavery was a terrible sin in America. The U.S. participation in slavery was a vile abomination against God and against the human race. It was as ungodly as many other atrocities against humanity that we see historically in other nations. Until just a little more than one hundred and fifty-five years ago, slavery was sanctioned and promoted by the U.S. government. What a travesty!

The slave trade in America was criminal. We are glad for the efforts of Abraham Lincoln and multitudes of others who resisted it and passed laws to stop it. Still, laws of segregation and oppression existed in the United States until recent decades. Although we have come a long way, racism and bigotry is still eating away at the fabric of American communities. I am glad for those who continue to fight the oppression of any people in society.

Long after laws against slavery were established in the United States, murder, whippings, and the burning of homes and churches continued, especially in the South. Even today, many in the African American community are afraid of some people in the white community. Many are fearful of while police officers, or of any white man in a military or security uniform.

As difficult as it is for me to think about the vile crimes against humanity, in foreign countries, during my lifetime, it is equally difficult for me to think of racism, and crimes against the black community, continuing here in America today. How can these things be?

Some Repentance

In America, many people have repented for the attitudes and actions of their ancestors toward the black community. I have lived most of my life in Canada, and I did not grow up in a racially charged neighborhood. The city of Toronto was multiracial, and my best friends were people of different skin color and ethnicity. Still, on many occasions, I participated in gatherings of public repentance because of the abuse of various people groups in Canada and in the USA.

The groups of people we repented to, were First Nation Indians, the black community, and the Jewish community. Brothers and sisters did their best to be reconciled to each other. The people I know who participated in these services have a genuine love for all of God's people, regardless of color or ethnicity.

On those occasions, forgiveness was extended and strong friendships were built between different church families and communities.

I think that most people in America desire a land of equality. They want to live in a nation where poverty is broken, and respect is given to every man and woman, who will live as a law-abiding citizens.

There are many other crimes against God and man, of which America is guilty. One that quickly rises to the top of the list, is the shedding of innocent blood, which is commonplace in America, through the popular abortion industry.

Abortion is a Crime Against Humanity

The White House and the Supreme Court of the United States of America, are not the highest court for establishing the law of the land. The courts of heaven, and He who sits on heaven's throne, decide the law of the land.

No matter what the Supreme Court says on this matter, taking an innocent human life is a crime against humanity. Abortion is the taking of an innocent life, and God will hold the nation accountable for every precious life that is taken.

In 1973, abortion became legal in the United States of America, because of the Roe v. Wade, Supreme Court decision. Since then almost sixty million legal abortions have been procured in the USA. More than one million babies are killed every year and the question rises, how long will God allow this to continue?

If these babies were not humans, made in the image of God, perhaps it would be different. If God determined that a fetus was not alive before birth, perhaps it would be different. But those ideas are ridiculous; neither of them are true. Every baby is made in the image of God, and human life is present at the moment of conception.

The truth revealed in the Bible, declares that God is the giver of life, and from conception, a human soul is formed. Destroying the fetus, is killing a baby, and God tells us that curses come upon those who shed innocent blood. Abortion is an act of murder. It is breaking the sixth commandment, thou shall not kill.

The Bible makes a distinction; all killing is not murder. Murder is the shedding of innocent blood, or taking a life when you have no authority to do so. A policeman, a judge, or a soldier can take a life, only if and when, the law warrants it. If a person kills another as an act of self-defense, where their life, or the life of another is clearly threatened, that is also a legitimate reason to kill someone and that is not murder.

Taking the life of a preborn baby, however, is most definitely murder. A tiny child in the womb is the most innocent of humanity, and God will hold the person who does such a thing, responsible.

If a nation promotes or sanctions, the act of abortion, then the whole nation will be judged. America is guilty of this heinous crime, and God is just in judging her for it.

A Global Judgment

Almost fifty million babies are killed because of abortions around the world every year. The curses have piled high over the nations and God will stop the carnage and judge those who committed it. The Bible tells us that the Great Tribulation, and the judgments that will come upon the earth during that seven-year period, are justified.

"The third angel poured out his bowl on the rivers and springs of water, and they became blood. Then I heard the angel in charge of the waters say: "You are just in your judgments, you who are and who were, the Holy One ... for they have shed the blood of your saints and prophets, and you have given them blood to drink as they deserve." And I heard the altar respond: "Yes, Lord God Almighty, true and just are your judgments." Rev. 16:4-7

Not Without a Reason

If the government made abortion a crime and people continued to have abortions illegally, the individuals involved would be judged. When that activity is endorsed by the federal government and the Supreme Court then, the entire nation is guilty of crimes against humanity, and the nation will be judged accordingly.

God's law supersedes all other laws. The great tribulation and its judgments are not without reason. The shedding of innocent blood, and the abuse and tyranny of other people, are terrifying dynamics in our society. They are not the only reason for God to judge America and the nations. Genesis 12, Deuteronomy 27, Ezekiel 22, and Malachi 3, give a biblical list of sins that result in curses. They include:

1. Witchcraft

2. Dishonoring parents

3. Abusing orphans, widows, immigrants and the poor

4. Abusing the handicapped

5. Business and financial corruption

6. Sexual perversions, including adultery

7. Assassinations of innocent people

8. Murder

9. Anti-Semitism

10. Not paying tithes and offerings

Daniel's Prayer

Those who love and fear the Lord, should pray the prayer of Daniel over America as Daniel prayed for Israel. If people repent and change, the hand of God can be stayed. Daniel prayed:

"O Lord, we and our kings, our princes and our fathers are covered with shame because we have sinned against you. The Lord our God is merciful

and forgiving, even though we have rebelled against him; we have not obeyed the Lord our God or kept the laws he gave us through his servants the prophets. All Israel has transgressed your law and turned away, refusing to obey you. Therefore the curses and sworn judgments written in the Law of Moses, the servant of the God, have been poured out on us, because we have sinned against you ... Our sins and the iniquities of our fathers have made Jerusalem and your people an object of scorn to all those around us. "Now, our God, hear the prayers and petitions of your servant ... We do not make requests of you because we are righteous, but because of your great mercy. O, Lord, listen! O Lord, forgive!"" Dan. 9:9-19

Chapter 24

Two Kinds Of Judgment

Judgments are Necessary

Judgment comes to those who break laws for two reasons. One is for punishment, because what we sow, we reap. People must pay when they hurt others. They must learn to think consequentially. Punishment also serves as a deterrent for others who are looking on. They will see that consequences follow behavior. Those who do well are rewarded, those who do evil are judged and punished. The lesson is, 'crime doesn't pay, it hurts, so don't do it.'

The other reason for judgment is redemptive. It is hoped that through judgment and suffering a person sees their behavior was wrong, and they decide to change their ways. The human heart can change and a person can be reformed. It may even happen that a vile offender has a conversion experience and instead of committing crimes, he defends and helps victims and the disadvantaged.

Some of the best ministers of the streets are those who used to be enemies of the state. They were abusers of themselves and of innocent people, but God turned them around and now they are social workers of the best kind.

John Newton

John Newton (1725-1807), was an evil slave trader, and the captain of a slave ship. It took a long time, but Newton gave his life to God and eventually left the trade. He wrote the song Amazing Grace - that saved a wretch like me. He became an abolitionist and partnered with William Wilberforce in the British Parliament to bring an end to slavery in England. He witnessed the British law to end slavery when it was finally passed in 1807, shortly before he died.

Saul of Tarsus

Saul of Tarsus (Paul the Apostle), was the most aggressive enemy of Christianity in his day. Before his conversion, he organized the public stoning of believers, and travelled throughout Israel, persecuting and imprisoning the followers of Jesus. He was so violent, that the entire church was afraid of him. Even after he came to Christ, they were wary of him.

Then, on the Damascus Road, as he was travelling with documents of authority, to detain and apprehend Christians, he received a judgment from God. Jesus stopped him on the road, judged him of persecuting the Church and blinded him on the spot.

He was led by the hand into Damascus where he repented of his sins. After three days God sent Ananias, to pray over him and he was healed from his blindness.

After, he was judged, punished and suffered for a brief time, Paul's life turned around. He became a powerful apostle, perhaps the greatest of all time, except for Jesus.

Two Kinds of Judgment

The Bible speaks of two kinds of judgment. One type of judgment comes to a person, while they are still alive on the earth. The second type of judgment comes, when that person stands before God or Jesus, in the afterlife.

"The sins of some men are quite evident, going before them to judgment; for others, their sins follow after." 1 Tim. 5:24

Judgment in Heaven

The first kind of judgment we will address, is judgment in heaven. When a person stands to be judged before God, in heaven, they stand alone. It does not matter what their father or mother did, they stand alone. And it does not matter what anyone else did to them along the way, they will be judged by what they did, or did not do.

They cannot say, "I was mistreated. That is why I was an evil person." They are simply judged according to what they did. They cannot blame anyone, and no one will come to their defense at that time. Nor will they be judged by someone else's behavior. Even if their father was Hitler, it will not be held against them on that day. They stand or fall on their own merit.

The book of Revelation tells us that there is more than one book that will be opened to expose them (See Revelation 20:12). One book is called, 'The Lambs Book of Life'. Your name must be written in that book if you are to receive your heavenly reward. It will only be there if you have repented and given your life to the Lord Jesus. The other books list the main aspects of your behavior. what you do and how you have acted during your life will be presented and God will judge you with mercy and grace.

The results of that heavenly judgment will be eternal. You have a heaven to gain and a Hell to shun. By the power of Christ's death on the cross, when you are weighed in eternity, may you be covered by His blood, and not be found wanting.

Judgments on Earth

God does not only give judgments in heaven, He delivers judgments on the earth, before people die as well. There is a great difference between judgments in heaven, and those that people receive while on earth. While those administered before God's throne are designated solely for an individual, those on the planet are a package deal. A family is judged for the sins of a father, and an entire nation is judged because of the behavior and actions of its government. That is one of the reasons why some families have reoccurring dilemmas, and some nations constantly fight abject poverty and disease.

This kind of judgment is called a curse, and in some cases it is a generational curse, because its effect extends for more than one generation. It always amazes me when I discover Christians who believe the biblical teaching of generational blessings, but refuse to believe the biblical teaching about curses. It reminds me of those who believe in angels, but not demons, and those who believe in heaven, but not Hell. We should not pick and choose verses in the Bible that we like while ignoring the ones with which we find difficulty. For a study on the subject of blessings and curses, I encourage you to read my book, '<u>Blessings or Curses for the Next Generation.</u>'

The prophet Jeremiah in chapter 31 tells us a time is coming when the sins of the fathers will not cause judgments for the children. A thorough examination of the text will reveal that this happens, when Israel come into the fullness of God's provision for her. Israel is far from the fulfillment of all things at this time. That does not come to pass until the millennium, of Christ's thousand-year reign on earth. As Jeremiah says, only then will generational curses come to and end.

America Pressures Israel

Judgments will come because of the sins of America. One of those sins is her failure toward Israel. Judgment because of this sin has already been documented.

There is an amazing book written by John McTernan called, 'As America has Done to Israel'. In the book, McTernan highlights the times when America has failed Israel.

As I mentioned previously in this book, since 1948, the United States has been Israel's greatest ally. There are many times since then, however, when the American government has put pressure on Israel to give up her land for the sake of peace in the Middle East. Every time the U.S. has done this, calamity has struck America. Is it a judgment from God? I think so.

Israel's purpose in the last days ranks high on heaven's priority list, and the United States has been assigned, by God, to stand with her. When the U.S. turns away from God's plan for the Holy land, a judgment hits America.

I am not sure that I agree with everything that McTernan suggests, but there is enough evidence to validate the general theme that if you mess with Israel, God will mess with you. Here are a few details that John McTernan highlights in his book.

"The National Oceanic and Atmospheric Administration (NOAA) monitors billion dollar disasters. NOAA identified forty-seven such disasters starting in 1992. ... America pressuring Israel over the covenant land is directly linked to twenty of these disasters ... The twenty totaled $334.8 billion in damages." [xxxiii]

Here are the twenty disasters to which McTernan refers, and America's pressure on Israeli to give up land for peace is connected with those disasters. This list ends in June 2006.

Hurricane Andrew, August 24, 1992 - cost $35.6 Billion - Hit on the same day the Madrid Peace Conference moved to Washington, D.C.

Arkansas tornadoes, started March 1, 1997 - cost $1.1 billion - Started the same day Arafat arrived in America to meet with President Clinton

North Plains flooding, the worst flooding in history - April 1997 - cost $4.1 billion - During Arafat's stay in America, and Clinton's sharp rebuke of Israel.

Hurricane George, September 23-28, 1998 - cost $6.5 billion - Clinton, Arafat, and Netanyahu meet to discuss peace plan. Arafat addressed the UN and received a rousing ovation as hurricane smashed US coast.

Texas flooding, October 1998 - cost $ 1.1 billion - Happened during the second meeting in Maryland with Clinton, Arafat and Netanyahu. Clinton was pushing Israel to give away 13% of the West Bank.

Oklahoma tornadoes, May 1999 - cost - $1.7 billion - The most powerful tornadoes to ever hit the USA. They hit on the same day that Clinton had asked Arafat to announce a new Palestinian State in Israel, with Jerusalem as its capital. Then complications arose and Clinton asked him to postpone the announcement until later in December of that year.

Hurricane Floyd, September 1999 - cost $6.5 billion - Israeli Foreign Minister met with Arafat's deputies to make arrangements for the "Final Status, " of Israel giving land away.

Western fires, July 2000 - cost $2.1 billion - Fires raged at the same time President Clinton, Israeli Prime Minister Ehud Barak, and Yasser Arafat met at Camp David, Maryland, to discuss giving away Israel's land.

Severe drought, July 2000 - During the same time drought compared to the Dust Bowl of 1934 - cost $4.2 billion in the West

Tropical Storm Allison, June 6, 2001 - cost $5 billion - On the same day CIA director George Tenet, sent by President Bush, was in Israel to stop the Israelis from building in the settlements.

National drought, March 2002 - cost $10 billion - Following the bombing of the World Trade Center on September 11, 2001, and during the next year, President Bush continued to speak of a two State solution in Israel. In his speeches, he said that America would take the lead and see that it happened.

Western fires, July 2002 - cost $2 billion - The US put extensive pressure on Israel to lift the quarantine of Arafat in Ramallah during a time of war.

Tornado storms, May 2003 - cost $3.4 billion - United States, Russia, European Union, and United Nations drafted a road map for peace.

Hurricane Isabel, September 2003 - $5 billion - The US blocked Israel from expelling Arafat, and the President met with King Abdullah of Jordan to discuss a peace plan.

Hurricane Charlie, August 2004 - cost $14 billion - In six weeks a record four hurricanes hit Florida (See next three hurricanes). This was unprecedented for any state in history. The total cost was over $40 billion - they came during a time of intense pressure from the US against Israel. President Bush pressured to divide Israel, and evacuate Israelis from Gaza. he offered $1 billion in loans to help the evacuation.

Hurricane Frances, September 2004 - cost $9 billion - (see Hurricane Charlie)

Hurricane Ivan, September 2004 - cost $12 billion - (see Hurricane Charlie)

Hurricane Jeanne, September 2004 - cost $6.5 billion - (see Hurricane Charlie)

Hurricane Katrina, September 2005 - cost $200 billion - This was the worst natural disaster in US history. It happened immediately following the time that President Bush pressured Prime Minister Arial Sharon to evacuate ten thousand Jews from Gaza and parts of the West Bank, Katrina hit and devastated the USA's southern shores.

Hurricane Rita, September 20, 2005 - cost $5 billion - this happened within one day of the final pullout of the four settlements in Samaria

Judgments Now

As John McTernan points out, the USA has received many judgments in recent years, because of her government leaders' sins. Her failure toward Israel is a glaring example.

As America continues to run away from God and fall asleep in the boat, her national sin will increase. Unless dynamic, godly change comes to the U.S., the judgments of God will increase and they will reach a level far worse than what we have known.

Pray for God's mercy, and a quick wake-up call, so that godly change will come sooner rather than later.

O Lord, move in power on behalf of your people. Come and wake up your church!

Chapter 25

Jonah Overboard

Certain Death

"Then the Lord sent a great wind on the sea, and such a violent storm arose that the ship threatened to break up. All the sailors were afraid" ... "Then they took Jonah and threw him overboard" ... "But the Lord provided a great fish to swallow Jonah, and Jonah was inside the fish three days and three nights." Jon. 1:4, 15-17

Fear of death, and fear of God, was stronger than the madness of the maelstrom. The sea had set its wrath against them; it was bent, with all its might and will, on killing them. The boat tanked from one side to the other, and in the chaos, the sailors saw the sea shake its hoary head. They knew that neither they, nor their ship, would survive the night. All would be ripped to pieces before this anger and fury relented. How could boards and limbs continue against the unyielding onslaught that churned against them, with such vengeance and malice? The waves pounded, like gigantic hammers. Every minute, tons of water leapt through the air, from the massive swells, and came crashing down upon the boat's vulnerabilities. As if searching for the vessel's weakness, it aimed its weaponry, blow-by-blow, at the planks and battens of the mariner's, miniscule toy. The unruly tempest threw the vessel against the rollers, like an overused rag doll, and the downpour was so heavy, that it felt, as if billows of added waves were falling upon them from the sky. They were caught in the grip of nature's ever tightening net, for the sea, and its God, had devised an unbreakable conspiracy against them. There was no escape. They raced, to no avail, against time, and the elements, but the sea could not be deterred. It was set by divine order, on killing them, and leaving only splintered remnants of their existence, in the wake of its fury.

The sailors had done all they could. They had tied the riggings, battened the hatches, and secured the hold. As the storm progressed, they threw their cargo into the sea, to lighten the load. The tempest grew worse, and they cast every tool and every necessary provision from their store, into the sea. They called upon their gods for mercy, and they did all they could, until all was done, that could be done.

Only the crew and the ship itself were left, and they looked at one another and said, "Who is responsible for this plague? Who has brought such death upon us?

No one, not even Jonah, thought that his sins warranted such devastation. All were guilty, but not guilty enough to draw a punishment of this magnitude. Someone, however, on this ship, must be so vile, and so evil, that even the sacrifice and loss of all provisions, and the combined prayers of the entire human manifest, could not quell the judgment that must be due.

And Judgment Fell

When a seafaring vessel is in grave peril, the captain must do all, within his power, to find a solution that renders the least amount of damage, or loss, to the people, ship, or cargo under his care. He has all authority, and the entire weight of souls, and property, rests upon him.

The captain had exhausted every resource, and from his perspective, he had no option, but to delve into the personal lives of the people, who were on board. Normally, he would not care where someone was from, or what they had done. He had a ship to sail, and did not need any extra conflict or drama. Live and let live, was his motto, but now he was pressed, to stand with the forces of nature and give out justice if it was needed. Perhaps there was a man of great evil among them. Perhaps the punishment, or even the death of one extremely wicked sinner, would satisfy justice, and the lives of rest of the crew and passengers, could be spared.

No one was stepping forward to confess his sins, so the sailors, with agreement from the captain, decided to cast lots to expose the culprit. All of the ancients believed in cleromancy, the casting of lots.

Small stones were marked, and thrown on the ground, or onto the judge's lap. Conclusions and decisions were determined accordingly. It was believed, that the falling of the lot was not random, but decided by God as it fell into position. It was God who determined the rolling of the die, the flipping of the coin, and the drawing of the straws. Even the Bible tells us that, **"The lot is cast into the lap, but its every decision is from the Lord." Pro. 16:33**

Everyone on board, took a turn, and the lot fell on Jonah. Immediately, he confessed that he was running from God. He told them, that God had sent the storm, and their only chance at survival was to throw him overboard.

The sailors were frightened even more, when they heard that Jonah was a Hebrew, and his was the God of heaven, the one who had created the sea. They tried everything they could to avoid hurting Jonah, but the storm only got worse. Although it was completely futile, they even made a last ditch effort to row the ship to shore.

Finally, the sailors cried out to God and prayed. They asked the Lord to forgive them for throwing Jonah overboard. Then they lifted him up in their arms, and cast him over the gunnels of the ship, and into the raging sea.

Immediately, the storm stopped, and the sea became calm. The fear of God, came upon the crew, and they made sacrifices of thanksgiving to the Lord. They committed their lives to Him, and made promises that they would live lives of righteousness, devotion, and kindness.

The Great Fish

What follows is how I imagine it to be for Jonah. He had been judged, but God was not finished with him. His judgment was not complete, and its purpose was not yet fulfilled.

Jonah, was caught, he was forced into a corner, and he finally admitted that he was guilty of running away from God. He could run no longer, so he gave up. He resigned himself to the fact that he was about to drown in a watery grave. It would soon be over, and he would not have to think about his failure, his sin, or his punishment.

Then, God provided a great fish. As Jonah hit the waves, something hit him. In the darkness, he caught a glimpse of the huge shape, and he saw the gigantic mouth open wide and engulf him. That is all he saw, for a darkness, blacker than any he had ever known, became his new environment.

At first he was shocked, he could not move, but strangely enough, he could breath. This monster had air from the surface in his gut and Jonah's head was lodged high enough to inhale it. Why wasn't he dead, and how long would it take for him to die in this God forsaken pit?

Jonah could do nothing to help his situation, so he just wished that death would come swiftly and without pain. Perhaps, he would run out of air, and fall asleep before the gastric juices would begin to eat away at his eyes and soft tissue. O, what a terrifying thought. He hoped this crazy horror would hasten to its end, and he and it, would soon be no more.

He prayed, "I am so sorry God. Please show me your mercy and compassion. Let me fall sleep. Take my spirit and my life, and let me open my eyes before your throne, washed clean and made new, in the sanctuary of heaven."

Then, the spirit of Jonah, exhausted and in shock, wandered off into a deep sleep.

He did not know how long he had been sleeping. It could have been days, but maybe it was just a few minutes. He was waking up, or was he still asleep. What kind of nightmare was this? "Where am I?"

He whispered it out loud, but he could not move. He strained his eyes, but he could not see, nothing at all, was visible, except in his imagination. The pressure against his body was completely restrictive, as if he was being held fast by a mindless, slimy monster. And the smell, o the smell, it was musky, and warm, and putrid, like nothing he had encountered before.

Then, suddenly, Jonah began to scream uncontrollably. He remembered the storm, the chaotic ship, and the terror of the frightened sailors throwing him overboard. He remembered the massive face, of the great fish that bolted toward him, and he strained his mind to imagine, what kind of creature it was.

His scream was a dead noise. It was muffled and it came back to him, instead of escaping from his mouth. He realized, he was in a nasty cavity, a cave, but one more dense than any on the surface. There were no air vents or movement here, he was in the belly of a monster fish and there was no leaving this place.

He lifted his arm and felt the silky smooth wet dome that was pushing down on the side of his head, and he wondered what would happen next.

What Was It?

The fish, for so the Bible calls it, was a provision of the Lord. God provided a great fish to come and swallow Jonah. It was sent to keep him alive.

Some researchers suggest it was a prehistoric Dunkleosteus fish - an extinct species from the arthodire, placoderm genus, which could grow to a length of thirty feet or more.

A Dunkleosteus fish could easily swallow a man whole, but the Bible suggests that the fish that swallowed Jonah, was vegetarian, and not carnivorous, like the Dunkleosteus. The fish had seaweed in its belly. Jonah says, **"The waters compassed me about, even to the soul: the depths closed me round about, the weeds were wrapped about my head."** Jon. 2:5 [Emphasis Mine]

A vegetarian fish would certainly have less acid in their gastric juices, allowing for a person to live longer in its stomach. If a person was in the stomach of a flesh eating fish, he would encounter much stronger digestive fluids, and he would have died, and been dissolved quickly.

The truth is, we can only guess at the possible fish or sea creature that might have swallowed Jonah. If God commanded a huge fish to swim alongside of the boat, in the midst of such a storm, that in itself would have been a miracle. Then, for God to direct a fish to swallow Jonah, at that exact moment he was thrown overboard, that would have been a miracle. If we believe in a God of miracles, then we can believe He could keep Jonah alive, and unharmed, for three days in a fish's stomach.

What Was Really Happening

Being in the belly of a great fish was a continuation of the Judgment that Jonah had to endure. There was a hidden agenda in the heart of God, that was unfolding during Jonah's deep-sea imprisonment.

1. God was dealing with Jonah as a Father deals with a son.

2. He was giving Jonah time to repent properly, and to adjust his thinking.

3. He was showing Jonah a new level of His sovereign power, so that Jonah's faith would increase.

4. He was teaching Jonah to be fearless.

5. He was teaching Jonah the power of prayer.

6. He was teaching Jonah the importance of absolute obedience.

When God was finished judging Jonah, Jonah was ready to turn the world upside down. He was ready to go to Nineveh, and by the time he got there, the people would be ready to hear what he had to say.

Chapter 26

Ananias And Sapphira Sunday

Band-Aids Will Not Heal America

No small Band-Aid-measure will heal America. A one-time judgment will not affect the United States, long-term. Like with Jonah, it will require an extraordinary series of supernatural events to change people's hearts and procure the purposes of God in the USA.

On September 11, 2001, the World Trade buildings in New York City, were demolished by terrorist. Although, this was an attack from a fanatical Muslim organization, many people in America looked at their own lives, and saw the need to draw closer to God.

For the next two weeks the churches around the USA experienced a surge in attendance. People were praying, some were repenting for their sins, and others were calling upon the Lord for mercy and protection. Although the attack was horrifying, the fact that many in the nation were turning to God, was good.

Even with the intense level of pain that hit America on 9/11, our national piety did not last. After just a couple of weeks, things returned to normal for most people. They stopped going to church, and although the attack on U.S. soil was so traumatic, it seemed to have little lasting effect on the majority of people's spiritual lives. In the end, folks were frightened and cautious, but not more spiritual.

Does that mean it will take a large amount of increased trauma to bring about a more permanent increase in godliness in the nation? I believe the answer is yes, it will take a lot of correction to change the spiritual course of America. It will require even more than an incident such as the devastating 9-11 terrorist attack, to bring about lasting change. I wish it were not so, but increased judgments are coming to the United States.

The House of the Lord

Judgment that will turn a nation back to God begins with the church. God's people must be zealous for righteousness, before we can expect unbelievers and sinners to step in line. This idea is not new.

Scripture says: **"If you suffer as a Christian, do not be ashamed, but praise God that you bear that name. For it is time for judgment to begin with the family of God; and if it begins with us, what will the outcome be for those who do not obey the gospel of God? And, "If it is hard for the righteous to be saved, what will become of the ungodly and the sinner?" So then, those who suffer according to God's will should commit themselves to their faithful Creator and continue to do good." 1 Pe. 4:16-19**

These are the words of the Apostle Peter. God used him to judge Ananias and Sapphira in the early church, as it was transitioning to become a force that would evangelize the world. These people were living in sin, and when confronted, they denied it. Then suddenly, they fell dead at the feet of the apostle. Judgment began with the family of God, and revival broke out in Jerusalem.

After Jesus died and rose from the grave, the Holy Spirit was given to His disciples, and the New Testament Church was born. It was amazing, every day, more and more people were added to their number, powerful miracles became commonplace, and people met together in homes to study, pray, and enjoy the presence of the Lord together. People gave whole tracts of land, and large amounts of money, as gifts to the Lord.

People cared for one another, and met each other's financial needs, and soon the gospel spread to the nations round about.

Sin Already

It was shortly after the birth of the New Testament church that sin found a way to pollute and disrupt the move of God. If left unchecked, it would open the door for demonic interference, and sin would stop the growth of the church before the gospel reached the Gentile nations. The Lord was not going to let it happen, so judgment came to the house of the Lord.

Ananias and Sapphira

Here are the details as recorded in the book of Acts.

"Now a man named Ananias, together with his wife Sapphira, also sold a piece of property. With his wife's full knowledge he kept back part of the money for himself, but brought the rest and put it at the apostle's feet. Then Peter said, "Ananias, how is it that Satan has so filled your heart that you have lied to the Holy Spirit and have kept for yourself some of the money you received for the land? Didn't it belong to you before it was sold? And after it was sold, wasn't the money at your disposal? What made you think of doing such a thing? You have not lied to men but to God." When Ananias heard this, he fell down and died." Acts 5:1-5

Ananias lied to the apostles, and the church, and ultimately to God; and God struck him dead. Soon after his wife came forward and stood before Peter. She did not know what had happened to her husband, and she lied, just as he had done. Immediately, she dropped to the ground, and died as well.

The fear of God came upon the whole church, and righteousness and holiness were restored to the congregation. God did not allow His baby church to become infused with financial corruption or lying at its very beginning. God will do it again.

Ananias and Sapphira Sunday

Before changing the nation, God will change the church. What will God do to insure holiness as the new, end-time, spiritual movement is birthed? As in New Testament times, I believe we will see <u>something like</u> an Ananias and Sapphira Sunday.

Today the church in America is largely polluted because of compromise and sin; it has become spiritually weak. Sexual sin, corruption, compromise, materialism, witchcraft, and a lack of love and passion for the Lord, and for people, are becoming more and more common.

Many pastors and church leaders are pouring out their lives and seeing very little fruit for their sacrificial labor. This is a product of sin. Instead of the zeal of God's house consuming His people, distraction is consuming them. Distraction has become so prevalent that even some of the best church members are shuffling around from congregation to congregation, without concern for loyalty or kingdom responsibility.

The strength of many is waning, and whole congregations are ebbing away as the church loses more and more ground in the nation. Instead of being a bright light to the world, we have become a bruised reed and a smoldering flax. It seems that all of the teaching, Bible study, and prayer, that some are faithful to maintain, is not enough to motivate the people of God to the level of commitment and zeal that is needed.

Worse than that, the apparent lack of the fear of God in the church has opened the door to gross sin. The church is being assimilated into the world and folks have become casual in regard to their faith. The devil's plan is to make the people of God an extinct species. Statistics show that he is slowly, but methodically, wiping us out.

The fear of God is the beginning of wisdom, and I think it will take a spiritual bomb to bring the fear of God back to the house of God. An Ananias and Sapphira Sunday, would be such a bomb.

This is just my idea but I put forth to you; Ananias and Sapphira Sunday! Watch for a day, sometime in the not so distant future, when many people literally die in church services, on one Sunday morning across the USA. It happened at the start of the early church and it can happen again, at the start of the end-time church.

With so many different denominations and so many disconnected churches around the country, one or two people passing away during Sunday service would hardly be noticed. The New Testament, Ananias and Sapphira-impact, could only happen if it took place in many churches, in many different parts of the country, and it happened all at the same time. Then people would take notice.

If it happened in enough places, say a few hundred places at the same time, the fear of God, would return to the house of the Lord. Overnight, people would turn from their wicked ways and begin to pray and seek God's face. They would begin to judge themselves, so that they would not be judged with the world.

God Changes Situations

I cannot say for sure that an Ananias and Sapphira Sunday will come, but God will do something powerful. We never exactly know how the Lord will change a situation, but the Bible narrative tells us that He does and He will, when His eternal purpose is challenged.

For example, when the early church was facing dark persecution, Jesus unexpectedly met Saul on the Damascus road. Saul, the worst offender, became Paul, God's greatest apostle, at that time. God turned the situation around in order to accomplish His purpose in and through His church.

Also, when the children of Israel were fleeing Egypt, they found themselves in an impossible situation. They were blocked in against the sea, but suddenly, God parted the waters. The situation changed immediately. The enemies of God were drowned, and God's people marched on toward the Promised Land.

We see God intervening again when Daniel was thrown into the lion's den. God shut the lion's mouths and rescued Daniel. The national situation changed, and decrees were sent from the king that all people, in all the lands, should worship the God of Daniel.

In ancient times, when the threat of genocide faced the Jewish population of Media-Persia, God used a young lady named Esther to win the favor of the king. Again, a hopeless situation changed and it had far reaching consequences. The word of God gained a foothold in that region of the world, and it lasted for hundreds of years, at least until the magi came to Bethlehem to worship the Christ child.

In the New Testament, when Paul and Silas were beaten and put in chains in the dungeon, God sent an earthquake and the jailer and his family were converted. Once more, God moved and the situation changed suddenly and dramatically. The church in Philippi was born, and God saw to it that strong influential families were founding members of it.

Persecution, entrapment, imprisonment, lions, genocide, and dark threats against God's people can be turned around in a moment of time. God continuously changes situations when His sovereign plans are at stake. He will do a powerful thing in America as well.

What do you think God will do to change the church? What will He do to change the world?

A Glorious Future

Look at this prophetic scripture that points to a future time:

"Arise, shine, for your light has come, and the glory of the Lord rises upon you. See, darkness covers the earth and thick darkness is over the peoples, but the Lord rises upon you and his glory appears over you. Nations will come to ... the brightness of your dawn." Isa. 60:1-3

This prophetic word is for Israel, but it is for all of God's Gentile people as well. When will the situation in the world change? These verses tell us, it will change during a time of great spiritual darkness. That level of spiritual darkness seems to be present in the world right now.

How will the nations change? Again these verses answer the question. The nations will come to the brightness of the people of God, because His glory will be seen upon them.

Suddenly, God will change the situation. He will change the world. He will change the nations. He will change its kings and rulers. They will come to the brightness of His glory; a glory that will cover and shine through the people of God.

It will happen unexpectedly and it will be so dramatic. The ominous question that remains is haunting many believers in America today. What is the thick darkness we will see before the glory of God comes to His people?

Chapter 27

America Overboard

Water in Your Face

Jonah was thrown overboard. He was immediately startled and shocked. He was hit by the thrashing waves, the massive monster fish, and its awful, slimy, peristalsis gut.

I remember the days when Joy and I were young parents. Our son would throw temper tantrums when he was corrected. We talked with him, spanked him, and we sent him to his room. Sometimes he would just hold his breath, and we did not know what to do. He would hold his breath for so long that we were worried that he might be causing some physical damage to himself.

When we took him for a scheduled medical checkup, Joy asked for advice from our family doctor. He told us that this was not uncommon, and suggested we throw a glass of cold water in his face when he held his breath like that.

Joy tried it. The next time our son was having a temper tantrum and holding his breath, she quickly got a glass of water and threw it in his face. He bolted back, gasped for air and started crying. The immediate problem was taken care of.

Jonah had a much worse shock than that. His body, soul and spirit were jerked back, when suddenly he was hit with God's judgment. Only God knows that the shock was necessary to produce repentance. The situation changed and Jonah embraced the call of God.

America is about to be shocked and startled at a level that will be so intense that she will not know how to cope with or process it. Eventually, the shock and judgment will jolt the people of America back to the plan of God

Possible Scenarios

Bible prophecies are so accurate. Revelation chapter six depicts the start of the great tribulation. It illustrates the first series of judgments that fall upon the earth, as the four apocalyptic horses leave the throne room of heaven.

They bring war, famine, and plague. Two thousand years ago, the Lord told the Apostle John that these things would happen to initiate the great tribulation. As I write, millions of Americans are worried that these exact things are about to strike our shores any day.

The threat of these traumas is constantly before us in the news. Few people, however, see them as judgments; they think they are just circumstantial. When they come, these judgments will be devastating and debilitating. And fight as we may, there remains in the psyche of the people, a deep underlying concern, that we may not be able to avoid or escape them.

Here are the three areas of concern that the prophecies foretell.

1. <u>Attacks from violent men</u>. (The Red Horse). This includes terrorists. There are planned terrorist invasions and lone-wolf attacks already in the works, against the USA. Every day we turn on the news and wonder if we will hear of another bomber or shooter who has attacked innocent people, here in the heartland of America. Most of these strikes, we expect to come from fanatical factions of Islam.

They are part of the first prophecy; the red horse judgments that will likely escalate into a worldwide, global war. It will be a war with the democracies of the world, fighting the dictatorships of the world. It will hit us hard, and millions of people will die because of it.

2. Natural or environmental disasters. (The Black Horse).This is the second prophecy of Revelation six. In the book of Matthew, Luke and Revelation, we read of droughts, and famines and other natural environmental disasters that will come in the last days. They include earthquakes, hurricanes, tornadoes, massive forest fires, asteroid showers, volcanoes, brutal hailstorms, and severe water shortages. Many of these catastrophic disasters are weather related and are seen as a result of global warming.

These are part of the black horse judgments of Revelation six. The Scriptures reveal that these global events will cause severe famines resulting in hyperinflation and economic collapse. Extreme food shortages will cause worldwide starvation and millions will die.

3. Plagues that include deadly global viruses. (The Grey Horse). The National Center for Disease Control, has been on high alert for years. The threat of a new, mutated virus, from swine, bird, or Asian flu, is very real. They know, if at any time, it gets out of control, they will not be able to stop its death march. The world cannot handle a super-flu epidemic.

In Revelation six, this is part of the grey horse judgment. It says that death and Hades follow this viral spirit horse. When it comes, it will be a nightmare. It will probably kill more people than the war and famine combined.

Abandoned by God

When these judgments come to America, the Bible promises protection for those who walk with the Lord. It also reveals that believers will be ministering care and compassion to the hurting people around them. The church will have its finest hour.

Many people will feel that God has thrown America overboard; as if He has forsaken and abandoned her. But to talk about these traumas, 'as judgments,' to the average person in America, is not politically correct at this time, and it will certainly not feel right to call them judgments, when they come. For a long time, it will not be fashionable to refer to these deadly events as judgments from God. Over time, little by little, people will begin to realize that indeed these are judgments. Then, they will cry out to the Lord for forgiveness and mercy.

God is gracious and compassionate and mercy and forgiveness is exactly what they will receive. Most of those who are not believers will suffer and many will die, but before dying, they will get right with God. Their momentary afflictions will be turned into a pathway to salvation. God will save their souls and bring them into His everlasting kingdom.

A Dramatization

In a previous chapter, I dramatized, what Jonah might have experienced when he was thrown overboard and was swallowed by the great fish.

The following paragraphs are neither history, nor prophecy. They simply reveal a made-up story of what a non-believer might experience as one of the judgments fall on America.

The Breaking Point- A Dramatization

"Well here I am, sitting down to write my next article," John thought to himself. "I can't keep up with the stories, but who needs to hear them, everyone has their own story. After a while, nothing seems surprising any more. You'd think the world was coming to an end or something."

"All this junk just can't last too much longer," he thought as he looked around at the massive, empty, office area. It was eerie, ninety percent of the people had been laid off since the tsunami wiped out the eastern seaboard. It destroyed the command center for Global News Network, several of their newspaper printing companies, and most of their telecommunication centers.

"Whew, we could have been there! I am so fortunate that our family was moved to Tennessee last year, so I could oversee the mid-west editorial department. There is not much left of it now. That move was just pure luck. Wow, fate, it works for some and not for others," John was muttering, in a whisper. Sometimes his thoughts came to him more clearly when he spoke them out loud, and anyway, he was all alone; no one was there to hear him.

The whole nation was in shock due to the 10-point earthquake that split open the ocean floor on the far side of the Atlantic. Eight hours later, the tsunami hit Manhattan. It took out the entire city; wiped it clean off the map. Because of smaller seismic tremors, they were expecting a big one days before it came. The early warning system allowed millions to escape. Still, hundreds of thousands of people, up and down the coast, never made it to higher ground.

Suddenly, the building where John was working, began to move. "On no, what's this?," he spoke in a louder voice. The building began vibrating erratically. John leapt from his chair and bolted for the stairwell. The shaking increased, and the walls began to lean and crack. "Not here! Not here in Tennessee, man the whole world is crazy. God, its falling apart."

John hurled himself down the flight of stairs, now jumping eight steps at a time. Then the whole building jerked upward and began to cave. Suddenly, the metal stair railing broke loose and thrust itself, like a warriors sword, across John's path. It struck him violently as he flew past, ripping open his kneecap. John was thrown against the far wall and tumbled forward, like a rag doll, to the landing below. "God, help me!" he screamed.

He felt like a wild animal in panic mode, who had suddenly, and unexpectedly, been caught in a trap. He was frantic. He pulled himself to his feet, but the building was still shaking uncontrollably, and he lost his balance once more, bashed his skull against a fallen beam, and fell, head-over-heels, several times, to a lower level.

Heavy dust had filled the space and he strained through stinging, watery eyes, just in time to see a huge piece of concrete drop from the ceiling. It landed right beside him, slid along his leg, then jolted forward, and came to rest lying across his abdomen.

John could not move, but through the billowing dust cloud, he noticed a pool of blood oozing out from under the rubble, onto the landing floor. The floor was now slightly tilted, and the blood was slowly moving in a small stream away from him. "Oh, my goodness, I guess that is my blood," he muttered through shaking lips.

He looked around, the broken stairwell was spinning, but so much dust was now filling his eyes, he could hardly keep them open. Then everything shifted to slow motion. His hearing became muted and muffled and dense, as if he was in a padded, sound chamber. He was in a daze and his life was hanging in suspended animation. Time and eternity stopped. It was unreal, and for a moment he wondered if it was only a dream.

No, this was not a dream, it was a nightmare. He pushed as hard as he could, but he had little strength, and the pile that pinned him down must have weighed several tons. "I am not making it out of this one alive," he thought to himself.

He leaned his head back on a shattered pain of glass and tried to catch his breath and gather what little coherence he could muster. He had always been smart enough to get out of the toughest situations. Surely, there was a way out of this one, he reasoned.

Then he looked up. It was difficult to see because of the dust, but he could make out parts of twisted metal and concrete hanging directly overhead. It looked like a huge mass of the broken building was dangling right above him, with tails and sticks, and bits still waving back and forth from the inertia of the fall. He knew the mass could break loose, and crash down on him, at any moment.

Suddenly, he experienced a surge of energy. He became more desperate, and with all of his combined might and will, he tried once again to free himself. He lifted and strained and pushed, but it was absolutely useless.

When he stopped his push and slumped back, he felt the life force drain from his body, like a huge down-surge of energy, similar to a great generator factory being shut down.

John lifted his head and yelled as loud as he could, "Help! Help! Can anyone hear me?" No one could, he was all alone. The whole city was in ruins and it would be days before anyone would find him. "On no," John thought, "I have met my match, I don't have long ... Here it is ... this is it. My time has come."

He thought of his wife Tammy and their six-year-old son, Raymond. "Oh, God help me!" He began to cry. He cried, and cried, and he repeated his simple plea, over, and over, and over again. "Oh, God, help me! Oh, God, help me! Oh, God, help me!" It seemed like that was all he could say for the longest time.

Twenty minutes must have passed by and John realized he had become very tired and a cold chill had come over his body. It was then he realized he needed to think about what he could do to prepare himself for the inevitable; he was about to die.

He worked hard at forming a thoughtful prayer. He had never prayed a thoughtful prayer - only a simple rhyming prayer before eating at his grandma's house when he was a kid. He had stopped believing in God more than forty years ago. Since then, he had been against the idea of religion. He even mocked church people, and promoted an anti-religious bias at the network. If anyone ever tried to talk to him about God or faith, he simply shut them down. There was no room for any kind of make-believe, of that sort, in his life.

"This was different now," he thought. "If this life is all there is, then everything is totally over for me. If there is more, however, well maybe, God is giving me a chance. I have heard about this before; God reaching out to someone in their last moments of life. Maybe, this is my time with God. I could have died instantly, but here I am. Oh God, this is so crazy!"

He began to pray, "I am sorry! I am really sorry! Please give me a chance. If you are really there, and if there is a life after this, Oh God, somehow include me. Please, help me!"

Suddenly, the entire stairwell filled with a brilliant light. There, in the bright light, standing before John, was a man in a white robe . "John, I am Jesus. Your grandmother has prayed for you, and I have heard her cry. John, I have heard your cry, and have come to bring you home."

Immediately, John began to weep uncontrollably, "Forgive me Lord, I have sinned so bad. I am so sorry. I did not know."

"It is alright. John, I forgive you." With that, John slumped back. His spirit left his lifeless body and both He and Jesus vanished. Only John's empty body remained.

It Is So Real

Although this was just a dramatization, this end-of-life scenario has happened, in different ways, thousands of times. I have personally talked with several people who have faced, near death experiences, and were saved after having a vision of the Lord Jesus. It happened to personal friends of mine such as Marjorie Hamilton, John Babu, and Marvin Rollins. In my own life, I have encountered supernatural rescues from certain death, on more than one occasion.

As judgment hits America, God will gaze upon the nation as the judge of all. No judge has ever been more fair, more merciful, or more compassionate. Judgments will come to a nation, because of its accumulated sins, but every person receives a fair trial concerning eternity.

The theme of the story I have told you is real. It will happen, over and over again, and all who call upon the name of the Lord will be saved. Most will not be saved from death, but many will be saved from an eternity in Hell fire.

Part 4

Rescue And Revival

Chapter 28

When All Hope Fails

Light in the Darkness

"When my life was ebbing away, I remembered you, Lord, and my prayer rose to you" ... "What I have vowed I will make good" ... " And the Lord commanded the fish, and it vomited Jonah onto dry land." Jon. 2:7,9,10

Jonah was suffocating in the dark belly of the great fish. All imaginable hope was gone, but Jonah was still alive. He was kept alive on God's supernatural, life-support system. Whether God sustained him with supernatural miracles, or he allowed the fish to swallow air on a regular basis to keep Jonah alive, we do not know, but Jonah was alive.

The other day I witnessed a peculiar sight. I was down at the lake, and a silver bass was eating tiny bugs off the surface of the water. With every bite, half of his body was jerking out of the water. He looked like a mechanical piston going up and down. At times he even kept his entire head out of the water, as he swam in circles, on his side, his mouth open, vacuuming up the bugs off the surface of the water. I am sure that a great amount of air was going into his belly, along with the insects. I am not saying that Jonah's fish ate bugs, but somehow God had a way of seeing that air was in the belly of the fish, so that Jonah could breath.

Whatever Jonah's physical needs were, God supplied them. The one thing that was missing for Jonah, was light. There was absolutely no light in the belly of the fish. It was pitch black, and for a long time Jonah's soul was pitch black as well. His time on earth was finished, and his life was ebbing away.

The presence of God is compared to the light of the sun, that humans need and crave. Without it nothing grows, and people are lost. Without light people cannot defend themselves; they cannot find their way , or see what is coming. Nighttime is the time of fear for many people, and the darker it is, the more fear some people experience.

Darkness in the Wilderness

I have often taken groups of young people wilderness camping, in northern Canada. This is a place where bears and moose roam freely, and from time to time, they came into our campsite. On cloudy nights, when the light of the moon and the stars were blocked, it became so dark that we could not see a thing.

We were sleeping in tents, and that meant that only a thin layer of nylon cloth separated the camper from the wild world of the forest. Some nights we would lie there and hear a rustling movement outside, in our campsite. We would lay still for a while then, if it persisted, we would grab a powerful flashlight, unzip the tent, and shine it in the direction of the noise.

Usually it was just a raccoon, but it could be a bull moose, or a black bear. Sometimes we had to deal with a wild animal. Usually they would run off, as we came out of our tents. It was essential to keep a clean campsite, free of food scraps. We had to tie our food in backpacks, on a high rope, between two trees or the bears would get them.

After hearing noises, getting back to sleep was not always easy, and we had to trust that we would be safe. We always were. Some folks, however, could not handle the fear of the unknown in that situation. The dark wilderness would be more then they could cope with.

A Deeper Darkness

There is a much deeper problem, than the darkness of the forest. It is the darkness within the hearts of people and it is always there. The dark, hollow cavity of an empty soul that does not know the Lord, can be a horrifying place. That is real darkness.

Years ago, I was saddened to hear the story of the late Michael Jackson. The famous rock star had died of a drug overdose. A medical doctor was injecting him with a drug, similar to one used on the operating table, during surgery in a hospital. When the drug was injected, the one who received it became unconscious. They would be in such a deep sleep that they would remember nothing of the night. There would be no fear, no worry, no panic, and no turmoil. It seems that Michael Jackson had to turn it all off, or he would have no peace from what was troubling him.

Something went horribly wrong and the prescription administered killed Michael. He never woke up this side of heaven. We do not know why Michael had this drug administered, but the only reason I can think of using such a dangerous procedure, would be to escape the darkness of the night. The darkness of a soul without the power of Christ, can be horrifying. Even believers who have not claimed their blessings can be full of fear.

A New Light Dawns

In the belly of the great fish, a spiritual light began to glow. Jonah was a man of God. Although he was running from God, he was God's friend, and he knew how to reach out and find Him.

Jonah prayed; I am sure he repented, and in time the light of God filled the belly of the fish. Amazing, but Jonah was not lonely anymore. He spoke to God and God spoke to Him.

If God can be with Jonah in the belly of a fish, in what place on earth, is it possible for God not to find someone? He can respond to any cry, from any place, at any time.

Scripture says:

"Where can I go from your Spirit? Where can I flee from your presence? If I go up to the heavens, you are there; if I make my bed in the depths, you are there. If I rise on wings of the dawn, if I settle on the far side of the sea, even there your hand will guide me, your right hand will hold me fast. If I say, "Surely the darkness will hide me and the light become night around me," even the darkness will not be dark to you; the night will shine like the day, for darkness is as light to you." Ps. 139:7-12

Darkness Over America

From the very start of God's end-time judgments over America, a darkness will engulf the nation. Many people will die, and millions will lose their homes and jobs. Those without Christ will struggle and fight for survival. Short-term solutions will help some people for a while, but as chaos continues, the darkness will grow and new traumas will emerge.

Listen to the Scriptures that describe these times.

"I watched as he opened the sixth seal. There was a great earthquake. The sun turned black like sackcloth made of goat hair, the whole moon turned blood red, and the stars in the sky fell to earth ... the sky receded like a scroll, rolling up, and every mountain and island was removed from its place. Then the kings of the earth, the princes, the generals, the rich, the mighty and every slave and every free man hid in caves and among the rocks of the mountains. They called to the mountains and the rocks, "Fall on us and hide us from the face of him who sits on the throne and from the wrath of the Lamb! For the great day of their wrath has come and who can stand?" Rev. 6:12-17

"The Forth angel sounded his trumpet, and a third of the sun was struck, a third of the moon and a third of the stars, so that a third of them turned dark. A third of the day was without light, and also a third of the night." Rev. 8:12

As with Jonah, the darkness over America, will be haunting. The experience, though terrifying, was not the end for Jonah, but the start of a new beginning. That is what will happen in the United States as well. A light will break through the darkness and the end-time Church will be born.

Chapter 29

The Beginning Of Birth Pains

Fearful Christians

As I write this book, I am aware that I have never seen a time when I saw so many Christians who are fearful. It is due to the warnings of prophets, and the great disparity, that God's people seem to have little or no training to prepare themselves for this time. Furthermore, their timeline is off due to incorrect teaching. The terrible day of God's end-time judgment is approaching, but it does not happen immediately. As I write this book, the day of doom is supposedly coming within a month. That is what some prophets say, but it will not come so quickly.

Some say that the end of all things is upon us. Their arguments are convincing, because scriptures are quoted, current events described, and historical, time-line patterns are illustrated with graphs and charts. Some speak about the seven-year cycle of restoration, or judgment, known as Shemitah. Others refer to Blood Moons, and some claim astrological calculations that point to a phenomenon called planet 7X.

The Shemitah

Those who refer to the Shemitah, note that every seventh year is a Sabbath year, and the ground must be left fallow. In the fiftieth year, seven Shemitahs have been completed, and all debts are cancelled. If God's people live in sin, then the Shemitah will not be a blessing, but a judgment. The charts of these prophets show that, throughout history, great calamities, and major blessings for Israel, happened at the end of the Shemitah year.

America is not Israel, and we must be careful not to put God's specific word for Israel on Gentile nations (see Col. 2:16). Still, the history of the U.S. seems special. It seems to be tied to the Shemitah. Major events in U.S. history can be traced to the Shemitah year. This year, as I write, is a Shemitah year, and it ends in September. So will end-of-the-world, catastrophic judgments fall on America, and around the world? Although the timing is off the principle is sound. I am confident that the seven years of the great tribulation will start and finish according to God's principle of the Shemitah.

Blood Moons

Adding to the message of Shemitahs, is the teaching of Blood Moons. Many preachers point to Scriptures that speak of end-time judgments that will hit the earth, before Christ's return. Three Bible verses speak about the moon turning red like blood. The moon is eclipsed when the earth blocks the sun's light from hitting it, causing it to appear red. That is why they call it a blood moon.

There were four lunar eclipses that fell, on the Jewish feast days of 2014 and 2015, and the final one happened on the Feast of Tabernacles, on September twenty-eight. Four lunar eclipses, landing on the Feasts of the Shemitah year, are rare. Teachers point out that whenever this has happened, world-shifting events have occurred. The biblical judgments connected with a blood-red moon, are catastrophic. They include earthquakes, famines, world wars, and economic collapse.

Other Science

Adding to the teachings of Shemitah and Blood Moons, is the, not so popular, teaching of planet 7X. The proponents of this teaching say they have scientific proof that there is a planet, hidden from view. They say, it has caused many of the global, biblical, and historical anomalies that are recorded in Scripture. Furthermore, the massive asteroids, brimstone, and deadly acid rain, mentioned in the Book of Revelation, will be caused by the gravitational pull, and the accompanying debris associated with the comet tails of this planet.

According to their calculations, this celestial body will get close enough this year to cause climate and geological catastrophes on planet earth. Then, they say, in March of 2016, a part of the comet's tail will strike the earth. This would bring about the end of the world as we know it. The question is, can so many prophets be wrong?

The Lesser Judgments First

The end-time, catastrophic judgments described by these prophets are definitely coming, but not immediately. Those global judgments are coming because we read of them in the book of Revelation. This, however, is not that day, and this is not that time. First, the lesser judgments must come.

Jesus said, **"You will hear of wars and rumors of wars, but see to it that you are not alarmed. Such things must happen, but the end is still to come** [the end is not yet]. **Nation will rise against nation, and kingdom against kingdom. There will be famines and earthquakes in various** places. All these are the beginning of birth pains." Mt. 24:6-8

Jesus exhorts His children, not to be afraid. He says, a season of lesser judgments will hit America before the ones mentioned in Revelation come. He also tells us that during this time something will be born. It is the powerful end-time church. We will discuss this further in future chapters, but as I write this book, we are still in the time when the lesser, but still intense judgments, come. Here is a further explanation.

Revelation chapter 6 says, **"I watched as he opened the <u>sixth seal.</u> There was a great earthquake. The sun turned black like sackcloth made of goat hair, <u>the whole moon turned blood red</u>, ... Then the kings of the earth, the princes, the generals, the rich, the mighty, and every slave and every free man ... called to the mountains and the rocks, "Fall on us and hide us from the face of him who sits on the throne and from the wrath of the Lamb! For the great day of their wrath has come and who can stand?""** Rev. 6:12-16 [Emphasis Mine]

Blood Moon Teachers, Jump the Gun

There are only two different incidences mentioned about a blood moon in the Bible. The one we have just read is from Revelation 6:12, and the other is Acts 2:20, where Peter quotes Joel 2:31.

Acts 2:20 says, **"The sun will be turned to darkness and <u>the moon to blood</u> before the coming of the great and glorious day of the Lord."** Acts 2:20 [Emphasis Mine]

The verses in Acts 2:20 and Joel 2:31, tell us what happens before the glorious day of the Lord. Revelation 6:12, tells us exactly when the end-time, blood moon judgments come. They happen when the sixth seal is broken. Logic dictates, that the sixth seal cannot be broken until the second, third, fourth and fifth seals are broken first. They bring war, famine and plague, and Revelation 6:8 tells us that two billion people will die when the first four seals are broken.

It is impossible for a world war, a global famine, and worldwide plagues, to come, and kill a quarter of the people on the earth in just a couple of months. The teachers who threaten such immediacy are jumping the gun.

The great tribulation has not yet begun, and it must begin before the extreme judgments happen. The blood moon event cannot come until after the first seals are broken. They have not yet been broken, so the ultimate judgments of the blood moon are still in the future. And, by the way, Scripture says nothing of four blood moons, we just need one.

On the day of Pentecost. Peter says, 'this is what Joel spoke of', and he quotes three amazing things (see Acts 2:17-21).

1. The outpouring of God's Holy Spirit upon all flesh.

2. Signs in the heavens, such as a blood moon, and fire and smoke, before the great and glorious day of the Lord.

3. And every person who calls on the name of the Lord, shall be saved.

On the Day of Pentecost, we see, at least a partial fulfillment of Joel's prophecy. The first part of the prophecy was the outpouring of the Holy Spirit. The third part of the prophecy was also fulfilled. For the first time in history, three thousand souls were saved, baptized and added to the church.

The middle part of the prophecy includes fire, smoke and the moon turning to blood. If that is yet to come, it lines up with Revelation 6:12, because that is the time prophesied for global destruction, and cataclysmic judgment.

The Lesser Judgments Have Begun

Catastrophes will come, but to start with, they will not be at the level of the Revelation judgments.

Many Christians are very afraid of complete global, economic collapse, but that is also shown to come during the great tribulation. Before then, the economy of the world will remain relatively strong. It is shown to unravel in the book of Revelation, so it has to remain significant prior to that time. There will be times of great financial loss, but worldwide financial collapse does not begin until the four apocalyptic horses are released.

Prepare Yourself Properly

Many judgments have already come to the U.S. and they will continue because of her sins. In recent years, she has experienced dozens of natural disasters, and I believe, many have been judgments from God. They are in response to our government and Supreme Court's legalization of abortion, pressuring Israel to give up land, and other national sins. This past summer, America changed the definition of marriage allowing gay couples to marry. The sanctity of life and marriage comes from God, and judgments fall on nations that attack the sanctity of life, marriage and family.

Right now, Christians seem to be frightened, about great financial loss or total economic collapse. But should they be? Jesus said: **"Do not worry, saying, "What shall we eat?" or " What shall we drink? or "What shall we wear?" The pagans run after all these things, and your Heavenly Father knows that you need them. But seek first his kingdom and his righteousness, and all these things will be given to you." Mt. 6:31-33**

During the first series of lesser judgments, it is not wrong to prepare, by storing some food and water, and being wise with your investments, but don't hoard, thinking that your security will come from that.

The promises of God hold true regardless of trials, national judgments, or tribulation. He promises that your food, drink and clothes are sure.

The Light of the World

As national judgments come, Christians still have an amazing calling to be the light of the world. In fact, our calling and purpose will only be sharpened during this time. Jesus told us to occupy until He comes, not to hoard, or hide away in fear. God's people are called to be overcomers.

People in the world may be full of fear because they do not know the Lord, but disciples of Christ are called to shine with righteousness, peace and joy. They have the Spirit of power, love, and a sound mind.

So, people of God, if you are here when the lesser of the great judgments come, rise up and shine and serve the Lord with gladness. Minister with Holy Spirit anointing.

Chapter 30
A Personal Revival

Shine Jesus Shine

"The people walking in darkness have seen a great light; on those living in the land of deep darkness a light has dawned." Isa. 9:2

This word from the prophet Isaiah, refers to the coming of Jesus as the Messiah, over two thousand years ago. The Spirit of Jesus is still here today, and people are still seeing His great light. When revival comes, it is this very light of Christ that will shine in the hearts of people, and that is what will change their lives.

"For God, who said, 'Let light shine out of darkness, made his light shine in our hearts to give us the light of the knowledge of the glory of God in the face of Christ.'" 2 Cor. 4:6

It will not be a political program, a federal law, or economic breakthrough that will save the day. It will be the revelation of Jesus Christ, the Son of the Living God that will bring us back to life. It will be just as supernatural as the day when God created the world. At that time God said, 'Let there be light', and out of darkness, the light came. He will say it again, and light will shine in the hearts of people. Let there be light over America! It will come like the rising of the dawn.

It does not matter how bad someone has been, what matters is the change of heart and actions by the power of God's Holy Spirit in a person's life. With man it is impossible to be saved, but with God all things are possible.

My Conversion

I remember what happened, the day my life turned around. I repented of my sins and gave everything to God. I was just fourteen years old, and I had rejected God, the church and the supernatural.

I was travelling, by myself, on a Grey Coach bus toward my home, after visiting a friend in another city. My friend was a believer, and although I had been raised in the church, I certainly did not believe.

The events of my visit brought the issue of God and salvation to the forefront. Before long I found myself talking to God and it seemed that He was speaking to me, in my mind. At first I did not know what to think. If God was real, I would be crazy to resist Him. On the other hand, if He was a fable, I did not want to live a life of pretend. I would not do that.

I was raised in the church, so I knew, if I was to pray to God, I would have to get serious. I decided to give my live completely to God, for one week. If He proved Himself to me, beyond my feelings and emotions, before the week was over, then I would commit the rest of my life to Him.

I started with the sinner's prayer. On the Grey Coach bus. I bowed my head and whispered a prayer that only God could hear. I verbally thanked Jesus for dying for me on the cross. I asked Him to forgive me of my sins and come into my life.

Suddenly, I had a remarkable experience. I look back at it now, and I know it was the Spirit of God coming upon me. The experience was so powerful that I immediately felt full of amazing ecstasy.

I opened my eyes and looked out of the bus window. Wow, it was as if someone had taken dark sunglasses off of my eyes. The world was so bright and the colors were so vivid. I had never seen the world like this before.

After the Dust Settled

Hours later I arrived home. A lot had happened during those hours and my heart and emotions were completely transformed. I felt clean and whole for the first time in my life. I felt happy and I had an amazing peace and joy inside of me.

I went to my bedroom and got down on my knees. I said, "God, this is the best day of my life. Please forgive me for any doubt, but I have to know this was not just an emotional experience. Within the next seven days I ask you to prove to me that you are real."

As the week progressed, I began to be chided by my older brother and sister, Andrew and Grace. They wasted no time in making fun of my so-called salvation. I could not talk to them about it, so secretly, I began to pray for them. They became the main focus of my prayers, and by the next Sunday, I was asking God to save them.

That was the seventh day of my conversion and I asked God to prove Himself to me by saving Andrew and Grace before the day ended. I said, "God, I know you will not force them, but you can pull them so hard that they will not be able to refuse."

The Sunday morning service came and went, but nothing happened to my brother and sister. I spent the day in prayer and told my mom I was not eating, because I was praying about something.

When God Moves

The evening service came and we had a guest speaker at the church. Halfway through the service, I looked back at my siblings, from my place on the front row. It did not look good, they were taking and ignoring the preacher, like always. I just prayed all the harder.

After the preacher had delivered his sermon, he asked who would like to give their lives to God. No one shifted, so he sat down and my father, who was the pastor, stood up to close the service. I kept praying.

Suddenly, the guest speaker rose from his seat and apologetically, asked if he could speak again.

He gave another impassioned altar call, but again, no one responded. He sat down and my father stood to close the meeting and I kept on praying.

Then, it happened again, the guest speaker stood and asked to speak a third time. He said he could not help himself. He gave another altar call, but again no one responded, and I kept on praying. It happened seven times.

The fifth time he gave an altar call, the power of God became so evident that people began to weep all over the auditorium. I was crying and I closed my eyes and prayed like there was no tomorrow.

The altar call was given seven times, and when I opened my eyes, there was Andrew and Grace on their knees at the front of the church. They were weeping and their hands were lifted in the air. They had given their lives to God.

God had answered my prayer. He had proven to me that He was real and that He answers prayer. That night, in my bedroom, I prayed and dedicated everything to Jesus. For the rest of my life, I followed the Lord and since then, I have seen thousands of conversions.

Personal Light

Every time someone comes to Christ it is unique. Each person has a different story and God reaches them in a very personal way. Even when they get saved with a crowd of other people, at some large event, they are not just a number to God. Each is an individual human being who has just been won by a personal, loving God, who for years, has been reaching out to them. It is absolutely amazing.

Nothing in the world moves faster than light. Recently, a space probe photographed the planet Pluto as it shot past. NASA, sent it from earth, and it traveled more than twelve miles per second toward the distant, celestial body. Even travelling at that amazing speed, it still took ten years for the probe to reach its target.

After the photos were taken they were sent to earth on light particles. The photos arrived back at NASA headquarters four hours later. The speed of light is incredible.

When God shines His light on a human heart, the miracle of salvation is instantaneous. God, who called light out of darkness, when He created the world, is still calling light to shine. Now, His light shines in the hearts of men and women and the people who live in darkness see that light and they are transformed.

Light for Jonah and America

As Jonah experienced gross darkness while he was in the great fish, the people of America will be caught in a great darkness as well. A light shone for Jonah in his darkest hour; it will be the same for multitudes in the USA. God's light can penetrate the darkest corner, and it will, for revival will come to America. The end-time church will be born and it will begin with God's end-time nation.

Chapter 31

The Jonah Revival

Is He a Ghost?

"Then the word of the Lord came to Jonah a second time: "Go to the great city of Nineveh and proclaim to it the message I give you. " ... He proclaimed: "Forty more days and Nineveh will be overturned." ... When the news reached the king of Nineveh, ... he issued a proclamation ... "Let everyone call urgently on God. Let them give up their evil ways" ... When God saw what they did ... he had compassion and did not bring upon them the destruction he had threatened." Jon. 3:1,4,6,7,8,10

Jonah repented in the belly of the great fish, and after three days God caused the fish to vomit him up on Israel's shore. He could not believe he was alive, but he was, and he was resolute. Now, he was ready to obey the Lord and make his way to Nineveh. This is the way I see it. This is what happened, as Jonah obeyed the Lord and travelled toward Nineveh.

He cleaned himself up, gathered some essentials, and after a good night's sleep, began making preparations to travel to Nineveh.

The story of Jonah's death at sea was extremely dramatic and it quickly spread throughout the region. The mariners had returned to Jaffa, for they had lost all of their cargo, and most of the store and equipment needed to make the month long journey to Spain.

They had one main thing on their minds, their encounter with Jonah, the Hebrew prophet who had sailed with them. The storm was enormous, but when they threw him overboard, it stopped immediately. Furthermore, some said, they saw a huge fish come and swallow him at the very moment he hit the water.

In those days, fireside stories were the fabric of society. The reward of a hard day's work was to sit around with friends and see if anyone could think of anything interesting to talk about. It was the entertainment, the news, and the information hub of every town and village. Soon everyone was gathering to talk and hear about the maritime sailor's adventure at sea.

Within a week, the story rose to a new level of mystery and intrigue. A lot of people had seen Jonah. He was alive, and he had joined a camel caravan, and was headed in the direction of the northeast, toward the Fertile Crescent.

There was an unusual buzz of questions. Was the man they saw, really the same man that had been thrown overboard? Was it a ghost, or had this man been raised from the dead? What was his name and where in the world is he going in such a rush?

He was Jonah, the famous preacher, and whether he was a ghost or not, he was headed away from home, toward the land where the enemies of Israel lived. A lot of people knew him, or at least knew about him, and from a distance everyone was watching him; they were anxious to hear about his every move. But Jonah was not talking with anyone. An ominous dread hovered over him. People said he looked like the harbinger of death. Folks got out of his way, but they stared at him from a distance. They couldn't keep their eyes off of him, and many stood out in the road and watched him until he was well out of sight.

The Specter Has Come

It was weeks before Jonah entered the gates of Nineveh. They knew he was coming, for the stories of his journeys had reached the great city long before he did. And some of the stories had been mixed with tales of Israel in Egypt, and the wilderness and beyond. They had grown into fanciful imaginations of ghost armies and enormous angels of death.

Jonah had a fire pent up in his bones and people could see it in his eyes. They tried to avoid the horror of his gaze, and most of all, they feared what he was about to do and what he would say.

Many were thinking and saying, "The judgment of God has come. The end of the world has come. The prophet of our enemy has entered our gates. The specter from the sea is here."

The merchants and protectors of the great city who watched the portals and gates gave him entrance and leave, for they had received no word from their superiors to hinder him. Furthermore, no one felt ready to resist him, and no one wanted to be the first to feel the heat of his vengeance, or experience the terror of his wrath.

No doubt, their own soothsayers had warned them of this day. They had spoken of a spirit man walking through the streets releasing curses, judgments, disease and death. Now, he was here, they saw him with their own eyes. The people had nowhere to hide.

Please Don't Say it

The city was large; it was the capital city of Assyria. It had more than one hundred and twenty thousand people living within its walls. It would take three days for Jonah to walk its streets, announcing the judgment and fire of God that was about to engulf it.

The people were already trembling. They were convicted of their sins. They had not heard him yet, but they already knew that Jonah's words would be true and they would hit their target. The stories were too real and too frightening, and they realized they were guilty of the vile charges that would be levied against them. Judgment day had arrived and they were in a panic for survival.

Then suddenly, Jonah stood in a high place, opened his mouth and began to preach. His words erupted with the energy and spew of an angry volcano. **"Forty more days and Nineveh will be overturned."** he yelled. His long index finger jabbing like a dagger toward the sunbaked sky.

Before the first day of Jonah's preaching was over, people were already repenting. They were humbling themselves as best they knew how. The king wasted no time either. He quickly leads with personal repentance, wearing sackcloth, and making proclamations of national piety. People were weeping uncontrollably and crying out to God for mercy. They were confessing their sins and making promises of restitution. A wave of Holy Spirit truth and conviction swept over the people like the massive waves of the sea in a violent storm. And God heard their prayers, and He saw their contrition.

God Forgave and Multitudes Were Saved

God will defend the disadvantaged and abused. It is not God's desire that any should perish, but He will not tolerate wickedness, especially when people call out to Him for mercy. His judgment falls on tyrants and thugs, whether they oppress a single person, or a whole civilization. The day of reckoning comes to all who bring violence and atrocities. It is God's nature, He cannot endure evil or injustice; His righteousness will always prevail.

Justice and correction are certain, but God knows our frame. He understands our depravity and our weakness and His mercy is always greater than His judgments. He gives an enormous length of time and opportunity for people to turn around and get things right. He even calls upon other people to pray for the wicked, so that He will have cause to intervene and rescue the vilest offender.

That is what he did to Nineveh. Someone, must have been praying. Someone, must have been crying out to God for mercy. Someone, must have known how to move the hand of heaven. From the king, to the beggar, the entire city repented and God saved them.

We cannot look into the hearts of one hundred and twenty thousand people, to see the level of their remorse or the seriousness of their grief, but God can. Evidently, there were enough people with enough godly sorrow and repentance, for God to change his mind and relent of His promised judgment.

Winds of Revival

Revival had come to Nineveh and it reached to many others in Assyria. Life and integrity flowed into the city where horror and death once lived, and some of the reforms that were made, lasted for decades. Peace and justice reigned and people could lift their heads, and live in safety. The Assyrians were not attacked by their enemies for many years to come, and the nation of Israel was not attacked by them. The winds of revival had come, but Jonah struggled with his part in it.

Jonah had been so primed and empowered by God, that he could not unstring his bow, when the battle was over. He sulked, and wined, and complained, and it took awhile for God to bring him around.

God loved Jonah and was proud of his participation, and he spoke to him as a Father speaks with a son.

"The Lord said, ... "Nineveh has more than one hundred and twenty thousand people who cannot tell their right hand from their left" ... "Should I not be concerned about that great city?"" Jon. 4:10-11

Chapter 32

Revival In Israel

Scripture Tells the Story

This chapter gives us a clear picture of what the Bible teaches us about the coming end-time revivals. We read about these revivals in Zechariah, and in the Gospels, and also in Revelation 7, and Revelation 14.

Redemptive Judgments

"Then I heard the number of those who were sealed: 144,000 from all the tribes of Israel." Rev. 7:4

A Jewish revival will come at the beginning of the great tribulation. It would appear that all the tribes are included in that revival and those saved in the nation will be represented by a symbolic number, 144,000.

Just as revival came to the impossible city of Nineveh, it will come to every nation at the end of the age (see Revelation 7:9). Before we look at the revival that is coming to America, it will serve us well to explore the upcoming Jewish revival. The USA has been connected with Israel, by God. As Israel goes, so goes America; and as America goes, so goes Israel.

The great tribulation-judgments, prophesied in the book of Revelation, are not punitive, but redemptive and they bring us to revival. That is why the judgments last for seven years. They will be devastating, but they are not all encompassing, or without hope.

God could speak the word, and the earth would be consumed in a flash, but He will not do that, because He loves people. Through the process of devastating judgments, He will bring billions of people to repentance and salvation.

It is true that many will go to a Hell, but Hell fire was not created for people. Hell was created for the devil and his angels. People go to Hell because they are vile and wicked, and because they persist on turning away from the Creator and His Christ.

During the seven years of the great tribulation, billions of people come to the Lord. After each series of judgments, massive revivals follow. We read:

"After this I looked and there before me was a great multitude that no one could count, <u>from every nation, tribe, people and language</u>, standing before the throne and in front of the Lamb. They were wearing white robes and were holding palm branches in their hands. ... Then one of the elders asked me, "These in white robes – who are they, and where did they come from?"... And he said, "These are they who have come out of the great tribulation: they have washed their robes and made them white in the blood of the Lamb." Rev. 7:9, 13-14 [Emphasis Mine]

Two Great Revivals

Here are some interesting facts from Revelation chapter seven.

1. There is a great Jewish revival in the tribulation period (symbolically 144,000 Jews are saved).

2. There is a massive revival of Gentiles during the tribulation. They come from every nation on earth.
3. The number of Gentile Christians saved during the first part of the tribulation period is so large that no human can count them.
4. Jews and Gentile saints are one in Christ, but the Jewish identity is preserved.

For the remainder of this chapter we will look at the Jewish revival and in the up-coming chapters we will look deeper at the American and international revivals.

One Hundred and Forty-four Thousand

Revelation seven reveals two great revivals. First come the 144,000 (a symbolic number) of redeemed Jews. God's mark of protection is put on the foreheads of the 144,000. Numerology is the study of numbers and the Bible has a definite numerology woven into it. One hundred and forty-four thousand is a number that symbolizes the great family of God. The number twelve stands for family or nation and twelve times twelve is 144. Jesus chose twelve disciples to be with him as his earthly family. God chose the twelve tribes of Israel to be his chosen nation.

The city of God in Revelation 21 is a picture of the bride of Christ, the family of God. Its dimensions are twelve thousand stadia, in each direction. It has twelve foundation stones and twelve gates. The leaves of its trees will bear twelve crops of fruit, which are for the healing of the nations. The number twelve seems to be everywhere. That is because it represents God's family, city or nation.

Twelve times twelve equals one hundred and forty-four. Multiply that times One thousand and it gives us one hundred and forty-four thousand.

That is the expanded number of a great family. The family of God is also a city. One hundred and forty-four cubits is the thickness of the walls of the city. The city of God is a family.

The Jewish Family

The first mention of one hundred and forty-four thousand refers specifically to the Jewish family who are part of God's larger family of Jews and Gentiles. The entire family incorporates redeemed Jews and saved Gentiles. They are the two branches of the olive tree mentioned in Romans eleven. The Jews are the natural branches and the Gentiles are the wild olive branches.

"If some of the branches have been cut off, and you, though a wild olive shoot, have been grafted in among the others and now share in the nourishing sap from the olive root… If you were cut out of an olive tree that is wild by nature, and contrary to nature were grafted into a cultivated olive tree, how much more readily will these, the natural branches, be grafted into their own olive tree." Rom. 11:17,24

Just in case we are predisposed to think that Israel, mentioned here in Revelation seven, is only symbolic, God clarifies the matter. Some believe that the 144,000 refer to a so-called, but non-existent, spiritual Israel made up of Gentile believers, but the Lord identifies each of the twelve tribes by name.

It would be a gross mistreatment of scripture to try to spiritualize these names and eradicate natural Israel from the pages of the book. This has been done throughout history, but I would not want to be guilty of mishandling these verses. The fact that these are real Jews is very important to God. He records their names emphatically. They are Israelites indeed, who have become followers of Jesus during the great tribulation.

Twelve thousand Jews, (a symbolic number) will be saved from each tribe. The fact remains that all the tribes are included, except for the tribe of Dan. As Judas was eliminated from the twelve disciples and replaced by another, perhaps Dan has been disqualified from the twelve tribes of Israel and replaced by another. Some believe this happened because his tribe chose to remain in idolatry. We read of this in the book of Judges.

"The Danites rebuilt the city and settled there. They named it Dan after their forefather Dan, who was born to Israel. There the Danites set up for themselves idols. They continued to use the idols Micah had made all the time the house of the Lord was in Shiloh." Jdg. 18:30

Lost Tribes?

Some contend that all twelve tribes do not exist anymore. Only God knows and no person can make that assumption. For centuries, thousands of Jews have changed their names to escape persecution. Their lineage is no longer traceable to man, except through DNA testing. It is likely that many people in the world are Jews, at least in part, but are unaware of it. God knows who they are. Like lost orphans who find their true parents later in life, many Jews will discover their identity in the end.

Israel's Folly is Not Permanent

Although we will not devote much time to this theme, it is necessary to clarify this next point for some Christians. The Jews fell from God's grace, but they will be restored. After coming to Christ, they will play a significant role in the tribulation period.

Israel wandered from the ways of the Lord through unbelief and hardness of heart (Rom. 11:20). She further departed from following the Lord when she rejected her Jewish Messiah, Jesus. The Jews, as a whole, lost the kingdom of God for a season of time. We read of this in the book of Matthew.

Jesus said to the Jews, **"The kingdom of God will be taken away from you and given to a people who will produce its fruit." Mt. 21:43**

The kingdom of God was taken from the Jews and given to the Gentile church, but that is not the end of the story. The book of Romans highlights the painful judgment that fell upon Israel.

"Some of their branches have been broken off ... they were broken off because of unbelief." Rom. 11:17,20

The story regarding God's chosen people continues.

Isaiah says, concerning Israel, **"Can a mother forget the baby at her breast and have no compassion on the child she has borne? Though she may forget I will not forget you! 'See I have engraved you on the palms of my hands; your walls are ever before me.'" Isa. 49:15**

Romans says, **"Again I ask: Did they stumble so as to fall beyond recovery? Not at all!" Rom. 11:11**

In the early days of the tribulation period, during the first series of judgments, revival will come to the nation of Israel. A symbolic, 144,000 will stand as evidence of a huge ingathering of Jewish believers.

Jewish Revival

A massive Jewish revival is prophesied throughout scripture and preached by saints throughout history. It will happen in the end times, just prior to the return of Christ. This is indicated in the book of Luke. Here, Israel is pictured as a fig tree.

"Look at the fig tree and all the trees. When they sprout leaves, you can see for yourselves and know that summer is near. Even so, when you see these things happening, you know that the kingdom of God is near. At that time they will see the Son of man coming in a cloud with power and great glory." Lk. 21:27,29

Romans, gives more details about the Jewish revival.

"I do not want you to be ignorant of this mystery, brothers, so that you may not be conceited: Israel has experienced a hardening in part until the full number of the Gentiles has come in. And so all Israel will be saved, as it is written: 'The deliverer will come from Zion; he will turn godliness away from Jacob. And this is my covenant with them when I take away their sins.' For God's gifts and his call are irrevocable." Rom. 11:25-29

Scripture tells us that a huge number of Gentiles will be saved and after that a great multitude of Jews will be converted. God has not forgotten His people. He will fulfill all of His promises to them. His gifts and call toward the Jewish people are irrevocable.

Furthermore, we read in Zechariah about the up-coming Jewish revival. The Lord says, **"And I will pour out on the house of David and the inhabitants of Jerusalem a spirit of grace and of supplication. They will look on me, the one they have pierced, and they will mourn for him as one mourns for an only son."** ... **"On that day a fountain will be opened to the house of David and the inhabitants of Jerusalem, to cleanse them from sin and impurity." Zec. 12:10, 13:1**

It will be a sovereign act of grace that will lead the Jews to sorrow, supplication, and salvation. They will weep when they finally realize that

Jesus is their Messiah. They will pray the prayers of supplication. It is likely, that millions of Jews will be saved during the tribulation period.

Church Fathers Speak Up

Throughout history, many of the church fathers preached about a Jewish revival at the end of the age. The following historical quotes are taken from the book, "The Puritan Hope; Revival and Interpretation of Prophecy," by Iain H. Murray.

Jonathan Edwards, a revivalist of the "Great Awakening in American", wrote, *"Nothing is more clearly foretold than this national conversion of the Jews in Romans eleven."* [xxxiv]

Can you imagine what will happen to the Church around the world when multitudes of Israelites receive Jesus as their Messiah?

Romans eleven, verse fifteen says, **"If the casting away of them be the reconciling of the world, what shall the receiving of them be but life from the dead."**

When revival comes to Israel, the Church will also be invigorated to new life.

The early Puritans believed this. They said, "The Scripture speaks of a double conversion of the Gentiles, the first before the conversion of the Jews, the second after the conversion of the Jews."

Thomas Boston of The Church of Scotland also preached this message. A sermon recorded from 1716 declares, *"Are you longing for a revival to the churches, then pray for the Jews. 'For if the casting away of them be the reconciling of the world; what shall the receiving of them be but life from the dead.' That will be a lively time, a time of great outpouring of the Spirit, that will carry reformation to a greater height than yet has been."* [xxxv]

In 1855, Charles Spurgeon preached the following, *"I think we do not attach sufficient importance to the restoration of the Jews. We do not think enough of it. But certainly, if there is anything promised in the Bible it is this. The day shall yet come when the Jews, who were the first apostles to the Gentiles, the first missionaries to us who were afar off, shall be gathered in again. Until that shall be, the fullness of the church's glory can never come. Matchless benefits to the world are bound up with the restoration of Israel; their gathering in shall be as life from the dead."* [xxxvi]

Jewish Revival Comes During War

Revival will come to Israel when the nations are gathered around her in a time of war.
Read the book of Zechariah, chapter twelve and chapter thirteen, verse one, and discover the following truths.

1. Israel's revival takes place when Israel has been brought back to her homeland.
2. At that time, she becomes an immovable rock among the nations. That happened in May of 1948 and continues today.
3. The nations will conspire against her, but her leaders rise up with new strength.
4. God protects Israel supernaturally and all who attack her injure themselves.
5. During that time when tanks are in motion and missiles are exploding, God will lift the veil from her eyes.
6. The people of Israel will begin to weep, repent and pray as the grace of God floods over them.
7. The Holy Spirit will pour salvation over them and all the families with their wives, will mourn with repentance as they receive a revelation of Jesus as Messiah.

Not all Israel will be saved during this first revival, but God will be persistent with them. Right up to, and including, the time that Jesus returns, Jewish people will come to salvation.

Chapter 33

International Revivals

More Details

We have looked at the Jewish revival, but now we will revisit these Scriptures, and also look at the Book of Romans to discover more about the revivals that are coming to the nations.

Worldwide Revival

Immediately following the Jewish revival, the Gentiles will experience a revival as well. It will be so large that it is impossible for the people on earth to count the number of souls that are saved. In contrast to the first revival, these are not Jews, but people from every nation, tribe, and language.

The salvation of thousands of Jews will have a spin-off effect upon the rest of the world. Breaking news of revival in Israel will warm the hearts of Christians around the world and especially in America. Holy Spirit flames will become roaring fires as Christians witness the nation of Israel receive Jesus as Messiah. Great faith will fill the earth and a passion for Jesus and

His kingdom will launch the Church into a new level of action. No place will this happen more dynamically than in the United States of America.

Millions of supernatural testimonies will become the focus of the day. Every possible vehicle of travel will be busy as Gentile and Jewish ministers connect for the purpose of revival. Jews and Gentiles will preach the gospel of the kingdom in every nation. This revival will feel like resurrection from the dead. It is foretold in the book of Romans.

It says, **"If their** [The Jewish People] **rejection is the reconciliation of the world, what will their acceptance be but life from the dead?"** Rom. 11:15

Some are Sleeping

As I travel throughout the U.S. I discover an incredible number of Christians who do not attend church regularly. There are multitudes who still love God, but do not enjoy church life. I do not agree with this practice of not attending church, but there are reasons.

1. Many have fallen because of sin and as a result, they have become distracted from their devotion to Christ.
2. Others, have been wounded by church leaders, who are often more legalistic than merciful.
3. Multitudes, who are spiritually gifted have been overlooked by church leaders. They are given no opportunity to grow or function.
4. It is painful and exhausting to sit and listen to preachers whose ministry is not anointed.
5. Some Christians try for a long time to fit into a church, but eventually they feel as though they are drying up. Unfortunately, some decide to put organized church on the shelf.
6. Others, with better attitudes, simply do not have a spiritual church in their community.

The truth is, it may be wrong, but there are reasons why multitudes of believers do not attend church. Thousands of genuine Christians are part of a sleeping army that will rise again in the hour of God's power.

Revival is Prophesied

The great tribulation will activate the end-time church. When discouraged or distracted believers see the hand of God at work, they will leave their wanderings in the wilderness, be washed clean, and rise to stand at His side. Many will repent of lukewarm lifestyles, and God will forgive them and put a new fire in their souls. The great tribulation church will rise with unity as well as power, because leaders will function at a brand new level of spiritual anointing, and God's people will follow them. This will happen in every nation on earth.

"There before me was a great multitude that no one could count, from every nation, tribe people and language, standing before the throne and in front of the Lamb. They were wearing white robes." Rev. 7:9

They will come from every nation, even those countries, which at present, are hostile toward the USA. In nations where the Gospel of Christ is outlawed today, a paradigm shift will occur. People will come to Jesus in the worst of places, because of the mercies of God and the new revelation of Jesus.

An excited elder in heaven asked John who these people are that make up this huge multitude that no one can count. He answers his own question.

He says, **"These are they who have come out of the great tribulation; they have washed their robes and made them white in the blood of the Lamb." Rev. 7:14**

Global Revival

Revival will erupt in America and around the world as God's two historical witnesses, the Jews and the Gentile Church partner as one new man. The natural and the wild olive branches will function together. The first part of the great tribulation will leave the world in a lot of pain. Billions will be ready to repent and give their lives to God. There will be an open heaven over the earth, and the greatest anointing for salvation in history, will be released.

Many voices of sin, perversion, idolatry, greed, and ungodly entertainment will be silenced because of God's judgments. Many TV networks and media facilitators will no longer function. Hurting people will be hungry for God.

Mercy Ministries

It is not the judgments alone that will catch the attention of the masses; the love and compassion of the saints will soften the hearts of multitudes. The world will witness a great expression of love from Israel and from the newly empowered Gentile church. When people of the world have nowhere to turn, they will discover the love of God flowing through His people.

They will also see a powerful demonstration of supernatural signs and wonders. Miracles will follow the preaching of God's word and multitudes will fall on their knees before the God of heaven. This revival will be greater than anyone could imagine.

Church Buildings are Too Small

Church buildings will be too small and there will not be enough of them. Homes and stadiums will become the common sites for spiritual gatherings. Every day will bring new purpose and adventure for the spiritual soldiers of the cross. Finally, they will see the miraculous power of God at the level beyond anything that has happened in the scriptures.

The judgments of the tribulation are dreadful, but they will bring man's greatest blessings. For many, evangelism will become more important than human survival.

Christians will finally understand the book of Revelation, and they will rejoice. They will know that this window for salvation, like the door on Noah's ark, will soon be shut. For those who enlist in God's army, the joy of the Lord and the call of God to partner with Him in the harvest, will overpower every pain that they might suffer because of persecution.

China Experience

I remember my visit to China. My dear fellow pastor and friend Dennis Penner, and I traveled there to visit the church and to witness for Christ. In Xian, we met a friend who traveled with us and translated for us.

Every day we prayed for souls and met with many people. With only one exception, every person we witnessed to, opened their hearts to Christ. We led each in a prayer of salvation. We saw; genetic scientists, businessmen, doctors, engineers, university students, and even a communist soldier, surrender their lives to Christ.

Each day we saw God save people in China. I have traveled to more than 40 nations, but I have never experienced such an open heaven over a nation like I did there. There are more Christians in China than in any other nation in the world including the U.S.A.

"163 million* is both a large and a small number. There are now more Christians in China than in the United States, but this number still represent only about 12% of China's 1.4 billion people. As large as the Lord's harvest is in China, it has only just begun." [xxxvii]

After my encounter there, I can understand how ripe the harvest of the world will be during the tribulation period. We will witness worldwide revival. The evangelism explosion will fulfill Bible prophecy. The number of new Christians will be so large that no one will be able to count them. I can see billions coming to Christ.

Revival In America

In Revelation seven, an elder asks John**, "Who are these people who make up this multitude and where have they come from?" Rev. 7:13**

He answers, **"These are they who have come out of the great tribulation; they have washed their robes and made them white in the blood of the Lamb." Rev. 7:14**

Many Christians think of Revelation as a frightful time, but fail to observe the growing crowd in heaven, that we are told of, in Revelation seven. The Lord will receive His reward. It is called the latter rain, the massive end-time harvest.

I believe revival will erupt first in the USA. We have talked about the good and the bad of this nation. We have highlighted the strength and weakness of the church in America as well.

The truth remains that so many Christians are praying, and serving the Lord with distinction, in this country. Americans have given generously to the poor, protected and defended the weak all around the world, and sent missionaries to the nations. And something else that is very important to God; the United States has stood with Israel, when most other nations have abandoned her. God will surely use America for the end-time harvest.

'What you sow you reap', so the Christians of the United States can expect a great harvest for they have sown seeds for the harvest for many years. The full abundant return will come. And then revival will go forth from

America to impact the revival in Israel, and it will spread to the nations of the world.

A Party in Heaven

The angels and the elders in heaven will rejoice. The Church has to catch up with the heavenly perspective. Heaven anticipates the harvest of the earth, but most of the Church is stuck in fear of judgment, escapism and self-preservation. Look at what happens in heaven.

"All the angels were standing around the throne and around the elders and the four living creatures. They fell down on their faces before the throne and worshipped God, saying: 'Amen! Praise and glory and wisdom and thanks and honor and power and strength be to our God forever and ever. Amen!'" Rev. 7:11,12

The entire host of heaven has waited patiently, alongside the Almighty. Angels, elders, and the four living creatures are in unity with the Lord. When they see this harvest of souls standing with them in the throne room, the excitement will be absolutely electric.

This is why Jesus died. This great crowd of sons and daughters justifies the longsuffering that heaven and earth have endured throughout the ages. This is God's inheritance, the reward for which the Lamb shed his blood. God loves people; and as they stand before him in robes of brilliant white, all of heaven will fall prostrate to worship Lamb and the Lord God Almighty.

INTERESTING FACTS

Here are some interesting facts that we find in Revelation seven.

1. There is a huge revival among the Jews (symbolically 144,000 are saved.)
2. There is a massive revival of Gentiles, who are saved from every nation.
3. The number of new Christians is so large that no human can count them.
4. Multitudes of Jews and Gentiles are actually saved during the great tribulation.
5. A dramatic, but mature supernatural upgrade comes to the church around the world.
6. Jews and Gentiles are one in Christ, but the Jewish identity is preserved.
7. Together Jews and Gentiles evangelize the world.
8. Many new converts will die during the tribulation.
9. They will stand before God and receive their eternal reward.
10. The heavenly host fall down and worship the Lord when they see this amazing harvest of souls.

Chapter 34

The Greatest Revival Ever

It Gets Even Better

The end-time revival phenomenon is about to get even better. We will study Revelation fourteen and go through the Scriptures to discover the Latter Rain Harvest. It is a reflection of the amazing love of the Lord.

Can it Get Better?

I want to show you something better. Even though Revelation speaks of several end-time revivals, one is larger than all the rest. We have not spoken of it yet. We receive a glimpse of it in Revelation chapter fourteen.

"I looked, and there before me was a white cloud, and seated on the cloud was one "like a son of man" with a crown of gold on his head and a sharp sickle in his hand. Then another angel came out of the temple and he called in a loud voice to him who was sitting on the cloud, "Take your sickle and reap, because the time to reap has come, for the harvest of the earth is ripe. So he who was seated on the cloud swung his sickle over the earth, and the earth was harvested." Rev. 14:14-16

Two Sickles

Prophecy is like a bow, pulled back. It waits for perfect timing, a proper focus on the target and the action of release. Four prophecy themes have been recorded in the first half of Revelation chapter fourteen.

They are:

A prophecy about a new anointing for the saints.

A prophecy about the eternal gospel.

A prophecy about the fall of Babylon.

A prophecy about final judgments.

When the time comes for these prophetic arrows to be released from the bow, two great events will involve sickles as recorded in Revelation fourteen.

The first is the sickle of salvation. It will harvest those who turn to the Lord. It is used to extract the precious fruit of the earth. It is wonderful and it is about the greatest revival of all time.

The second is the sickle of cleansing. It will cut away the evil from the earth. It is the sickle of wrath and judgment. It is the sickle held in the hands of the proverbial grim reaper.

In this chapter we will only focus on the first sickle. It is a harvest tool, an instrument of blessings and revival.

Like a Son of Man

A new picture appears on the Revelation screen. John sees a white cloud and someone like the son of man sitting on it. The term, "Son of Man," is a title used in scripture, to describe Jesus. This, however, is an angel who is like the "son of man," it is not the Lord, but an angel. He is glistening white and shining like the sun.

He is an angel for we read, **"Then another angel came out." Rev.14:15**

God's awesome glory will shine through him. Two things about his attire stand out. He has a golden crown on his head and a sharp sickle in his hand. He is poised over the earth, waiting among the clouds. He is ready to initiate the biggest harvest yet.

Commanding Officer

Suddenly, another angel will come out of the temple. The temple is God's throne room. The angel will come from the presence of God Almighty, the Lamb and the congregation of heaven. He is an officer of the throne room. He will receive instructions from Jesus and proclaim it in a loud voice to the angel who sits on the clouds. His order will not be a secret; the entire spirit realm will hear him.

He shouts, **"Take your sickle and reap, because the time to reap has come, for the harvest of the earth is ripe." Rev. 14:15**

Three simple phases initiate the greatest revival in history.

1. The time has come

2. The fruit is ripe.

3. Take your sickle and reap

God is Patient

Harvesting the earth was in God's heart even before the world was formed. God wants His family at His side. That is His harvest. He waited patiently as man was created. Man had free will and he faltered and fell. According to plan, God sent His Son, redeemed the world, and began to harvest a family for eternity.

He has drawn mankind to Himself through the cross of Christ. The message of God's grace has gone around the world, and people of every nation have responded. No human need go to Hell because God's mercy overcomes judgment. Christ paid for man's sin.

Each person will be judged according to what he knows and what opportunities he has had to receive or reject the Lord. Those who understand more about the Lord, will be judged more severely than those who understand little. There are multitudes and millions of people who have been saved throughout history. A steady harvest of souls, have come to Christ. Only God knows how they came, who they are and how many there will be. God has been patient.

Now, at the end, the majority of people on the planet will come to Christ in a very brief season of time.

The Fruit is Ripe

At no previous time in history have all the nations come to such a corporate valley of decision. Never before has the veil of secrecy drawn back to expose both, the kingdom of darkness and the kingdom of God's dear Son. The anointing on God's people to evangelize the world has never reached such a powerful level and there has never been so many who are ready to receive the Lord. The fruit is ripe.

The spiritual environment of the great tribulation has brought the scorching heat and the heavy rains. Droughts, winds and calamity have all added their pressures to help prepare the harvest. The time has come.

The Latter Rain

The end-time harvest of the earth is known in scripture as the latter rain. In the Twentieth Century, a powerful movement and a season of revival was called the 'Latter Rain Movement'. The participants saw miracles, thousands were saved, and they thought they would usher in the great end-time harvest of souls and see the return of the Lord.

The Latter Rain Movement, came and went. It was a foreshadowing of the real one, and we can expect many more foreshadows before the coming of the real latter rain. Scripture talks about the former and the latter rains. Here are a few verses that validate this teaching.

"Therefore be patient, brethren, until the coming of the Lord. See how the farmer waits for the precious fruit of the earth, waiting patiently for it until it receives the early and latter rain." Js. 5:7 NKJV

"Be glad then you children of Zion, and rejoice in the Lord your God; for he has given you the former rain faithfully, and he will cause the rain to come down for you – The former rain, and the latter rain." Joel 2:23 NKJV

"Ask the Lord for rain in the time of the latter rain. The Lord will make flashing clouds; He will give them showers of rain, grass in the field for everyone." Zec. 10:1 NKJV

"Let us pursue the knowledge of the Lord. His going forth is established as the morning; He will come to us like the rain, like the latter and the former rain to the earth." Hos. 6:3 NKJV

"Then I will give you the rain for your land in its season, the early rain and the latter rain, that you may gather in your grain, your new wine and your oil." Dt. 11:14 NKJV

The latter rain is so powerful that the Lord uses it to describe His blessings and favor.

"In the light of the king's face is life, and his favor is like a cloud of the latter rain." Pro. 16:15 NKJV

The latter rain will come and the great harvest will follow.

The Earth is Harvested

"So he who was seated on the cloud swung his sickle and the earth was harvested." Rev. 14:16

The end-time revival is so massive that it deserves the title, "the harvest of the earth." The harvest does not mean the removal of people off of the earth, although many will die soon after they are saved, and their souls will go to heaven. Others, however will not die, but be present on earth for the second coming of Christ - both groups are part of the harvest.

Shortly after the halfway point of the tribulation, the massive revival comes. It happens so quickly, it is compared to the single stoke of a farmer's sickle. Millions of evangelists, many of them Jews, will share the testimony of Christ in every land. Miracles of healing and deliverance will follow the preaching of the gospel. The result will be the greatest harvest of souls in history.

During the first half of the tribulation many non-committed souls became believers. At the halfway mark, it seems impossible for many others to be saved, but not so, God has been working on them. The power of Jesus blood and the anointing of the Holy Spirit will save vast multitudes this late in time. the hardest of men's hearts will be softened and they will turn to God in a flash, in an instant.

We should never say that our community is too difficult for the gospel. We should never think that anyone is so defiled or so stubborn that they are beyond God's grace. God will prove that they are not.

While millions upon millions are converted to Christ, still many will refuse Him. They are the ones who choose to serve the Beast. Even many of them, will eventually come to Christ before the very end. Oh, the wonders of the riches of Christ! Even when times get there very worst, Christ's victorious cross will be saving souls.

A Testimony to the Nations

The Lord Jesus said, **"And this gospel of the kingdom will be preached in all the world as a testimony to all nations and then the end shall come." Mt. 24:14**

It is not just the salvation of souls that is at stake; the testimony of this revival is also significant. This one time global harvest is the high-point victory of the cross. The darker the evil, the brighter will be the works of God. Where sin abounds, grace does much more abound. The cross is more powerful than all the systems of the world. The testimony of the cross will be seen by all. Heaven will see it, the nations will see it and Satan and his demons will see it as well. Heaven will rejoice, the earth will be glad, but Satan will be angry and completely frustrated.

It is time that the church embraced a victorious eschatology. Understanding the harvest of the earth and the massive end-time revivals, allows believers to embrace hope and go forward into the future rejoicing.

What About Revival in America?

In the next chapter we will explore the subject of the up-coming revival in America. It will be unique. It will be incredible. It will be a fulfillment of destiny. Stand in the gap and intercede for this nation. Be part of the team that partners with heaven for God's special end-time nation.

Chapter 35

America - A History Of Revival

It was Foreshadowed

American prophets have often spoken of revival. The spirit of revival is felt in the famous Battle Hymn of the Republic. Although different lyrics were written much earlier, it was first published with its modern lyrics during the American Civil War.

Julia Ward Howe, submitted the lyrics she wrote to 'The Atlantic Monthly', and it was first published in the February, 1862 issue of the magazine.

The Battle Hymn of the Republic

Mine eyes have seen the glory of the coming of the Lord;
He is trampling out the vintage where the grapes of wrath are stored;
He hath loosed the fateful lightning of His terrible swift sword:
His truth is marching on.

I have seen Him in the watch-fires of a hundred circling camps,
They have builded Him an altar in the evening dews and damps;

I can read His righteous sentence by the dim and flaring lamps:
His day is marching on.

I have read a fiery gospel writ in burnished rows of steel:
"As ye deal with my contemners, so with you my grace shall deal";
Let the Hero, born of woman, crush the serpent with his heel,
Since God is marching on.

He has sounded forth the trumpet that shall never call retreat;
He is sifting out the hearts of men before His judgment-seat;
Oh, be swift, my soul, to answer Him! Be jubilant, my feet!
Our God is marching on.

In the beauty of the lilies Christ was born across the sea,
With a glory in His bosom that transfigures you and me.
As He died to make men holy, let us die to make men free,
While God is marching on.

(Chorus)
Glory, glory, hallelujah! Glory, glory, hallelujah!
Glory, glory, hallelujah! While God is marching on.

by Julia Ward Howe.

A History of Revivals

Long before the days of the Civil War, America experienced many explosive revivals. The following excerpts are taken from History of Revivals of Religion, by William E. Allen[xxxviii]

"The year 1790 ushered in a new era of revivals for the United States. Religion had sadly declined during the previous years."

"At this time there were no American Missionary societies, no Bible societies, no Tract societies, no Education societies. At home—religious indifference; abroad—the darkness of death over the heathen world."

"In 1790 there were extensive revivals in Pennsylvania and Virginia. "At this time," says Dr. Griffin, "began the unbroken series of American revivals." In New England, during four or five years, **about one hundred and fifty churches were blessed with Revivals.** [Emphasis mine]

This revival period continued for many years, and powerful revivals prevailed in New York, New Jersey, Pennsylvania, Ohio, Kentucky, Tennessee, the Carolinas, and Georgia."

Harlan Page writes of a revival in New York, "The Lord appears now to be coming down on all parts of this great city, to arouse His children and to awaken sinners. <u>Thousands of Christians here are praying</u> [Emphasis Mine] as they never prayed before. Conversions are occurring in all parts of the city. Churches are daily crowded to overflowing, and a most fixed and solemn attention is given to the dispensation of the truth."

"Christians at that time believed that, "The Church is the Bride of Christ, and the mother of his children." And that, 'No soul is ever converted except as some believer has painfully travailed in birth for that soul.'"

"The American Board of Foreign Missions, the American Bible Society, the United Foreign Missionary Society, and other missionary movements, were formed at this time as a direct result of the revivals.

During these years many colleges were blessed with revivals. Dr. Tyler wrote of Yale College having thirteen special revivals in a period of twenty-five years."

Early American Methodist Revivals

"The following article is taken from the "New History of Methodism," Vol. II., p. 106. "The early years of American Methodism witnessed an almost continuous revival. Scarcely a society was formed which did not grow out of a revival."

"American Methodism grew after this manner, in no period of the early history were revivals more general than during the years from 1784 to 1808. At one time all Maryland was ablaze with revivals. Similar signs and wonders were seen in Virginia. In New England revival followed revival, some of them of great power. In 1800 one of the most remarkable spiritual movements of American history began in Kentucky, and spread through Tennessee and Ohio with the amazing swiftness of a prairie fire." [xxxix]

Finney's Revivals

"Charles Grandison Finney laboured continually in powerful revivals." "In the Autumn of that year [1834] he delivered his famous "Lectures on Revivals of Religion." The reading of these lectures has resulted in hundreds of revivals in America and other countries.

Finney became Professor of Theology in Oberlin College in 1835." "Twenty thousand students came under his influence during the years he was at Oberlin. While still in connection with the College he conducted some of the most powerful revivals of his ministry".

"He emphasized that any company of Christians can have a revival if they will fulfill the necessary conditions; agonizing prayer, and a balanced presentation of the truths of the Gospel.

"The secret of Finney's power was the baptism of the Holy Spirit, and a life of prayer. He wrote, "In regard to my own experience, I will say that unless I had the spirit of prayer I could do nothing."

Revival in Rochester - 1830

"After receiving many pressing calls to preach, Finney felt that Rochester was the most needy."

"Soon [1830],there were some very marked conversions, one of the first being the wife of a prominent lawyer. The meetings became thronged with lawyers, physicians, and merchants. Many of the lawyers, became very anxious, and freely attended the enquiry meetings. It was in this revival that Finney began to use the 'anxious seat.'

The revival took a tremendous hold of the High School. Nearly every teacher and student was converted. As a result, forty of those students became ministers, and a large number became foreign missionaries. The majority of the leading men and women in the city were converted. Some years later Dr. Beecher talking to Finney of this revival in Rochester, said; "That was the greatest revival of religion that the world has ever seen in so short a time. **One hundred thousand were reported as having connected themselves with the churches as the result of that great revival**." [Emphasis Mine]

American Revival 1857-58

"Finney writing of this revival said, "This winter of 1857-58 will be remembered as the time when a great revival prevailed throughout all the Northern States. It swept over the land with such power, that for a time it was estimated that not less than **_fifty thousand conversions occurred in a single week_**." [Emphasis Mine]

There had been a daily prayer meeting observed in Boston for several years; ... A divine influence seemed to pervade the whole land. It was estimated, that during this revival not less than **_500,000 souls were converted in this country._** [Emphasis Mine]

There was such a general confidence in the prevalence of prayer, that the people very extensively seemed to prefer meetings for prayer to meetings for preaching. The answers to prayer were constant, and so striking as to arrest the attention of the people generally throughout the land."

"The following account of the revival was published in a journal at that time, "Such a time as the present was never known since the days of the Apostles, for revivals. Revivals now cover our land, sweeping all before them, exciting **the earnest cry from thousands**, 'What shall we do to be saved?' [Emphasis Mine] ... The large cities and towns generally from Maine to California are sharing in this great and glorious work. It really seems as if the Millennium was upon us in its glory.""

Key Factors

Several factors come to the forefront, when we think what happened to bring about America's revivals.

1. It was a dark time in history and the harvest was ripe

2. God raised up powerful leaders who won favor with the people

3. Agonizing prayer for souls was the main impetus and release for the revivals

4. Extraordinary preaching rose from the crucible of prayer

5. Many disciples were commissioned and released to preach salvation

6. There was a demonstrative release of Holy Spirit anointing

7. Revival spread to different denominations and missionary societies were raised up to send many ministers of the Gospel to the nations of the world

The revivals that took place in America during the Eighteenth and Nineteenth centuries were among the greatest that the world has ever seen. The fingerprints of God have always been on America.

What happened in the past was a foreshadowing of what will come to America in the future, and that which is coming will be so much greater in number and power than anything the world has seen before.

Chapter 36

America's Coming Revival

Can You Imagine?

If you have eyes to see, perhaps you can partner with God in prayer and witness the greatest revival this nation, and the world has known.

This chapter is prophetic. It is a foretelling for what, I believe, will happen as revival breaks forth in America. As the late Martin Luther King Jr. said, "I have a dream!"

Come With Me

Chaos and tribulation will shake America to its core. The end-time judgments of God will come. Terror attacks, natural calamities, plagues, and international wars will result in death and pain, and the church will go to her knees.

God is behind the tempest and the storm, and through it, He will lead us to repentance and restoration. He will cause the church to supplicate. He will lead her to the altar of intercession. Leaders will take their stand to preach, prophesy and proclaim repentance and revival.

At that time, Ananias and Sapphira Sunday will bring the fear of God back to the followers of Christ. People will weep, rededicate their lives, and fervently call on the name of the Lord. Prayer meetings will spring up all over the nation and people will spend as much time as they can calling upon the name of the Lord. Many prodigals will return to the Father and rise with new anointing and strength.

The heavens will open, angels will descend and multitudes of saints will receive dreams and visions from God. Miracles and amazing signs and wonders, will become commonplace within the family of God. The testimonies of supernatural healings and salvations will be evident and everywhere.

Churches Will Be Full

Churches will fill with capacity crowds within weeks, and souls who have never heard the Gospel will begin to come to Jesus. Some will come because they are grief-stricken, as so many family members and friends will have died.

Others will be full of fear and they will seek prayer for their sick and wounded friends. Out of desperation, they will ask for comfort and miracles. They will give their lives to Christ and become a catalyst for revival.

Still others will find their way to God's people because they had a vision of an angel or of the Lord Jesus, Himself. Some will have apocalyptic dreams and come to share them, as if they had an amazing thing to tell the Christian community. They will not know in advance that it will lead to their own conversion.

Preachers, both seasoned and new, young and old, will prophesy the day of the Lord, with great power and authority. Multitudes will come to Christ in every state and in every city.

People will hurry from work and rise before the day begins, to join with others who are pouring out their hearts in prayer. Nothing will be more important than prayer and prophetic worship. The worship will not be entertaining; it will be focused on the adoration of the Lord and on personal dedication to Him.

And You Shall Be Witnesses

There will be such an open heaven, that the workplace, schools, shopping malls, and streets, will become active mission fields. People will share faith stories, pray and prophesy over non-believers and many will be interested to hear and see what is happening. Christians will be bold in their faith once again and multitudes will come to Christ before they even enter a church.

They will be encouraged to go and hear the word preached. Meetings will be continuous as people and preachers, take their turns to hold the fort, and maintain the anointing. Morning, afternoon and every evening, preachers will take their place delivering the word. Both simple and deep, the apostolic, word of God, will reach the world.

Disciples, Disciples, Disciples

From house to house, the Holy Spirit will gather families and neighbors to study God's Word and pray.

A spiritual hunger will grow and young disciples will not be able to get enough of God's Word. Millions of people will teach and train the new and the young.

The process of spiritual reproduction will be phenomenal. After only a brief time of learning, new converts will be preaching to the next wave of souls who are receiving salvation.

Many influential and famous people will come to Christ. Politicians, celebrities, national sports figures, and leading business people, will give their lives to Christ and pave the way for national events and programs so they can share the Gospel of Christ extensively.

Gangs, criminals, the disadvantaged and displaced persons, will be among the first to come to the Lord. They will become some of the greatest ministers in the land. Ethnic minorities, people of the ghettoes, the homeless, the violent, and frustrated protestors, will experience a huge reformation. From hopelessness, they will rise to extraordinary faith, joy and supernatural strength. God will begin to turn their community situation around. Where there was no hope, hope will come like a river overflowing its banks. Community leaders will reach their own community and will call their people to Christ, and they will come by the hundreds of thousands.

Political Reformation

The Gospel will reach every stratum in society. Christian leaders will be elected to political office, from city councils to the White House. The people will call upon them for real change, and for the first time in years they will believe that godly change is possible in America.

Many politicians in America are already followers of Christ, but a bold shift will come at that time. Zeal and populous support will embolden national leaders to reach beyond political correctness. They will call the nation back to its Judeo-Christian roots.

Many ungodly laws will be overturned, and even the Supreme Court will have a change of heart. Issues like the preservation of life, marriage, family, drugs, sexual promiscuity, the poor and the immigrant, will reach new levels of godliness in America. Freedom will reign, but not a freedom that violates the wholesome and godly benefits of society.

All around the world the Gentile church and redeemed Israel will lead the nations in righteous reformation. The leaders of Israel and the Gentile church are the Two Witnesses that John recorded in Revelation eleven.

"'And I will give power to my two witnesses, and they will prophesy for 1,260 days, clothed in sackcloth.' These are the two olive trees and the two lampstands that stand before the Lord of the earth." Rev. 11:3-4

Great Joy for Some

Although Americans will still be reeling in the devastation of enormous calamities, the Great American Revival will bring immense joy to the nation. Peace beyond logic and an understanding of God's kindness and grace will be the living experience of so many. Laughter and joy, that was never known, will flow in many homes. From the flames of pain and sorrow, the fire of God will shine and the hearts of many people will embrace righteousness and rejoicing. It will be the order of the day.

Not everyone, however, will be happy. Even though millions will come to Christ, multitudes will harden their hearts and refuse God's grace. Anger will rise in the camp of the wicked and violent uprisings will be seen around the country. At that time, the terrorist will not come from terrorists groups of other nations, but from the ungodly among us. Their target will be godly politicians, churches, and the Christian community as a whole.

Abortionists, Gay activists, drug lords and crooked business people, will be furious over the righteous river that will be flowing in America. They will strategize, scheme, and devise, as much trouble as they can. The violent ones will be quickly subdued, but their animosity will continue to fester. For a further understanding of this backlash, I encourage you to study Revelation chapter eleven, and read my book, 'Unexpected Fire.'

"**Now when they** [The God-anointed politicians in the land] **have finished their testimony, the beast that comes up from the Abyss will attack them, and overpower and kill them. Their bodies will lie in the street ... For three and a half days men from every people, tribe, language and nation will gaze on their bodies and refuse them burial. The inhabitants of the earth will gloat over them and will celebrate by sending each other gifts, because these two prophets had tormented those who live on the earth. But after three and a half days a breath of life from God entered them, and they stood on their feet, and terror struck those who saw them. ... And they went up to heaven in a cloud while their enemies looked on. ... and gave glory to the God of heaven."** Rev. 11:7-13

The Revival Season

The massive revival in America will last for one to three years during the first part of the great tribulation. It will be birthed at the same time that Israel receives her great Messianic revival.

During the first half of the great tribulation, God will use these the two nations to spread revival to every nation, and people group. Every nation will experience their own revival, but I believe, it will start with America and Israel. (Study Revelation 7:9-13)

"**After this I looked and there before me was a great multitude that no one could count, from every nation, tribe, people and language, standing before the throne and in front of the Lamb. They were wearing white robes and were holding palm branches ... Then one of the elders asked me, 'These in white robes-who are they, and where did they come from?' ... And he said, 'These are they who have come out of the great tribulation; they have washed their robes and made them white in the blood of the Lamb.'"** Rev. 7:9,13,14

The people of God will rule and reign over the nations for a short while after the first great revival. Then the beast (The Antichrist) is allowed to kill them. They are resurrected and taken up to heaven. Because of that many more people come to Christ.

Then the Antichrist will become fully revealed to the world as we discover in Revelation chapter thirteen, and many people follow him.

This is the time of the great divide, for multitudes upon multitudes around the world will not follow the beast or worship his image. That will result in the greatest revival of all time as mentioned in Revelation fourteen. It is called the harvest of the earth. This will be the final great harvest before the Lord's return. Let us read the account.

"I looked, and there before me was a white cloud, and seated on the cloud was one 'like a son of man' with a crown of gold on his head and a sharp sickle in his hand. Then another angel came out of the temple and he called in a loud voice to him who was sitting on the cloud, 'Take your sickle and reap, because the time to reap has come, for the harvest of the earth is ripe.' So he who was seated on the cloud swung his sickle over the earth, and the earth was harvested." Rev. 14:14-16

Once the second half of the great tribulation begins, the most extensive revival in history will happen. After their salvation, most of those believers will become martyrs, and be taken up into heaven.

Not everyone will die or be taken, for we who are alive and remain shall still be on the earth to welcome the return of the King.

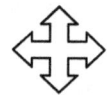

Chapter 37

America Makes The Millennium

Goats and Sheep

"When the Son of Man comes in his glory and all the angels with him, ... All the nations will be gathered before him, and he will separate the people one from another as a shepherd separates the sheep from the goats. He will put the sheep on his right and the goats on his left. Then he will say to those on the right, 'Come you who are blessed of the Father; take your inheritance' ... Then he will say to those on the left, 'Depart from me, you who are cursed, into the eternal fire prepared for the devil and his angels." Mt. 35:31-34, 41

The nations are compared to sheep and goats that a shepherd separates. The Lord looks at the populations of those nations and determines whether or not they will be in His millennial kingdom. If they are a sheep nation they are included. If they are a goat nation they will not be part of the new millennium.

We know that Egypt, for example, will be in the millennium. It is mentioned in Zechariah chapter 14 verse 18 as being a nation on the earth, during Christ's thousand-year reign.

Nations are judged by their leaders' choices and actions, but also by the godliness and prayers of her people. At the very end, Egypt will repent and turn to the Lord, and God, who is so merciful, will bring her into His millennial reign (Read Isaiah 19).

Christians who died will be resurrected to life at Christ's coming, and those who are alive and remain until His coming shall receive glorified bodies as well. They will reign with Christ, on the earth, for one thousand years. The rest of the dead, those who were not saved at His coming, will not come to life until the thousand years are over.

"They came to life and reigned with Christ a thousand years. (The rest of the dead did not come to life until the thousand years were ended.) This is the first resurrection. Blessed and holy are those who have a part in the first resurrection. The second death has no power over them, but they will be priests of God and of Christ and will reign with him for a thousand years." Rev. 20:4-6

The Nations

Throughout history, God formed the nations and gave them their allotted time (Acts 17:26). On the whole, they fell prey to the lies of the devil, and by the time the great tribulation arrives they will be excessively evil.

To give a further explanation, multitudes will come to Christ during the great tribulation, because the judgments will bring them to repentance. Soon after being saved, they will be killed by the enemy and transported into the presence of the Lord.

The majority of people who are still alive at the end of the tribulation will be sold-out servants of Satan. At that time, most Christians will have died, and most of the people who are left will receive the mark of the beast, and will worship his image. They will be an abomination to the Lord. God will judge them for how they have treated Israel, and for the many sins they have committed against Him and His Anointed One, and against innocent people. The Lord will destroy them and cast them into Hades where they will wait for the one thousand years to be over. Then they will be brought forth to stand before the great white throne, for God's final judgment.

Some Unbelievers Are Spared

While the vast majority of people belong either to the holy or the wicked, some seem to be caught in the middle. They will not willfully serve the devil, but neither will they follow the Lord. We discover that God does not destroy them.

When the Lord comes to judge the nations, some fence sitters will be allowed to live. The Bible speaks of them in several places and refers to them as survivors. They live beyond the second coming of Christ, and strangely enough, they enter the millennium along with the redeemed. They will be given another opportunity to be saved, because God is a just judge. Here are some verses that explain this, and help us with the big picture.

"The earth is defiled by its people; they have destroyed the laws, violated the statutes and broken the everlasting covenant. Therefore a curse consumes the earth; its people must bear their guilt. Therefore earth's inhabitants are burned up and very few are left." Isa. 24:5-6

"For with fire and with his sword the Lord will execute judgment upon all men, and many will be those slain by the Lord." Isa. 66:16

"Then the survivors from all the nations that have attacked Jerusalem will go up year after year to worship the King, the Lord Almighty, and to celebrate the Feast of Tabernacles." Zec. 14:16

"They will neither harm nor destroy on all my holy mountain"... "In that day the Lord will reach out his hand a second time to reclaim the remnant of his people." Isa. 11:9,11

The millennial crowd is a mixed bag, but God will give a second opportunity for salvation to more people than we might think. Note in the following verses, the thousand year reign, is also called the wedding banquet.

"The wedding banquet is ready, but those I invited did not deserve to come. Go to the street corners and invite to the banquet anyone you find. So the servant went out into the streets and gathered all the people he could find, both good and bad, and the wedding hall was filled with guests. But when the king came in to see the guests, he noticed a man there who was not wearing wedding clothes... Then the king told the attendants, 'Tie him hand and foot and throw him outside, into the darkness where there will be weeping and gnashing of teeth.'" Mt. 22:8-13

Jesus allows some survivors to enter the millennium, even though they have not believed in Christ. They will be given a second chance. Many undeserving will come to the great marriage supper of the Lamb. We read that both the good and the bad are brought in, so that the hall will be filled. Some refuse to wear the robes of righteousness and will eventually go to Hell after the millennium is over, and the great white throne judgment is complete.

Children are Welcome

Some ambiguous survivors, who attacked Jerusalem, are not the only ones who will enter the millennium as unredeemed mortals. Unborn children and many young people will also enter without glorified bodies. They had not previously known the Lord, or received the forgiveness of sins before His second coming. They were not caught up into the clouds to meet the Lord in the air when he appeared, so they did not receive glorified bodies.

This will happen because some will be in the womb of an unbeliever when Jesus comes. Some will be unsaved teens or children that the Lord will not send to Hell. Many more children will be born to these survivors during the millennium. Jesus loves children. In all of the synoptic Gospels, Jesus says 'let the children come to me and don't refuse them.' He says 'the kingdom of God belongs to children.'

"Let the little children come to me, and do not hinder them, for the kingdom of heaven belongs to such as these." Mt. 19:14, Mk. 10:14, Lk. 18:16

Jews With Abraham's Faith

Thousands of Jews with Old Covenant faith will be in Israel when the Lord comes and lands on the Mount of Olives. For all of their lives they were living a disciplined life of faith in God, according to the revelation they had. They followed the example and teaching of Abraham and Moses, and they were anxiously looking for the Messiah. They did not know Christ, so when He entered the clouds they were not caught up to receive glorified bodies with the saved of the nations.

When Jesus appears, however, they will immediately acknowledge that He is the Messiah they have been looking for. Because of this, the Lord will rescue them (see Zechariah 14:1-9) and bring them into the millennium. They will not have glorified bodies, but they will receive great blessings from the Lord. For an in-depth study of Jews in the millennium, see my book, 'Unexpected Fire.'

Hidden Believers in America

Many underground Christians will be alive, in America and in the nations, when the Lord returns. They will be incognito in every country, watching and waiting for the second coming, at the end of the great tribulation.

Groups of hidden believers will be all over the United States of Americas. They will be resilient, faith-filled, resourceful, followers of Christ, whom the Antichrist will not be able to dismiss, uncover, or destroy. They will be praying for and ministering to, many unsaved people, right up to the end. They are part of the woman's seed (the people of God - see Revelation 12) who are alive and remain until the coming of the Lord. We read:

"The woman was given the two wings of a great eagle, so that she might fly to the place prepared for her in the desert, where she would be taken care of for a time, times and half a time [Three and a half years - the last half of the Tribulation], out of the serpents reach. ... Then the dragon was enraged at the woman and went off to make war against the rest of her offspring- those who obey God's commandments and hold to the testimony of Jesus." Rev. 12:14,17

Israel will be the only place on earth where believers will still be open about their faith. Israel will have many enemies and the world will be at war with them. The Holy Land will be inhabited with redeemed Jews, Old Covenant Jews, secular Jews, and many Christian Gentiles. When the Lord comes to Jerusalem, He will rescue most of the people who live there. Many will be saved from wrath even though they did not previously accept Jesus as Messiah.

America in the Millennium

It is inconceivable to think that the USA will not be a sheep nation, because of her God-serving history, her end-time calling, and her many passionate, sons and daughters of faith. America will be included with the nations of the saved, in the great millennium.

By the time the nations march on Jerusalem, in the battle of Armageddon, the U.S. government will be following the beast, and the false prophet.

America will attack Jerusalem, because all of the nations will march against the Lord, and His chosen people, at that time.

For several years, prior to Armageddon, Israel will be attacked and, with God's help, she will defend herself. Because of this Israel will grow in size to engulf all of Lebanon, Jordan, Syria, and parts of Egypt, Turkey, Saudi Arabia, and Iraq (see Genesis 15:19-20).

The United Nations will command Israel to, "Give that land back." Israel will refuse, and as a result, the nations will muster their armies, and march on Jerusalem. That will seem to be the logical, human reason for the battle of Armageddon. Actually, the attack will be a demon-inspired battle.

The Millennium Begins

At that time the Lord Jesus will come. He will destroy His enemies, and His millennial reign will begin. America will be there. Those who have served the Lord with distinction, will be given special blessings. Godly individuals from every nation, will become kings and priests, and will lead and rule over the nations of the earth.

The nations will look to Israel as the hosts, administrators, and worship leaders, for all who come to the homeland and throne-room, of the King. Jerusalem will be the capital city of the world. Jesus will live and rule from there, and the people of the nations will worship Him. The nations will be rebuilt and all will live in righteousness and peace.

Chapter 38

America In The Millennium

The Nations Bring Their Glory

During the millennium, all countries, including America, will be called the nations of the saved. Each chosen nation will be rescued from extinction, to be ruled by the most valiant, sons and daughters of the Living God.

Then the nations will bring their glory and honor to the Lord. They will walk in the light of the temple and bring their blessings and gifts to God in Jerusalem. Scripture says:

"The nations of those who are saved shall walk in its light, and the kings of the earth bring their glory and honor into it. And they shall bring the glory and the honor of the nations into it." Rev. 21:24,26 NKJ

Every nation has a special and distinct destiny given by God. Some are peacemakers, others are inventors. Some nations are rich in the arts, and others reflect amazing gifts of service, worship, leadership, athletics, hospitality, farming or business administration.

During the millennium, all countries will have experts in all realms of life, but each will excel with some distinction, a skill that is superior to that of other nations. Each nation will be known for their own excellence and they will come and bring their best to the Lord.

Like individual people, each nation will reflect a beautiful aspect of the glory and character of God. No person has the full measure of God shinning through them; they must partner with other saints to see a display of glory that even approaches God's.

The nations likewise, will partner with other nations to demonstrate and illustrate God's glory. The heavens declare the glory of God - and so do people and nations. We are not told that every nation will be in the millennium, but I believe that most will be resurrected for the new world. America will certainly be there.

We know that people from every nation and language are already in heaven. Jesus purchased them with His blood, and their nationality and ethnicity are recognizable as they stand before God's throne (see Revelation 7:9).

Uncovering The Glory of the Nations

"On this mountain the Lord Almighty will prepare a feast of rich food for all peoples, a banquet of aged wine – the best of meats and the finest of wines. On this mountain he will destroy the shroud that enfolds all peoples, the sheet that covers all nations; he will swallow up death forever. The Sovereign Lord will wipe away the tears from all faces; he will remove the disgrace of his people from all the earth. The Lord has spoken." Isa. 25:6-8

The Lord will take away the shroud that covers the nations. This shroud hides their inherent talents and gifts. Today many people disregard America's exceptionalism. But God has established it. Her fight for freedom, compassion, aid to the poor, and her righteous pursuits, have been second to none.

Presently, people and nations are robbed of their identity, their destiny, and their godly heritage. All of that will change in the millennium; then, they will shine with God's glory.

The nations will be reformed for the new millennium. The dark shroud will be removed from them. Then they will bring their special grace, honor, talents, distinctions and glory to Jerusalem. I will be proud of America on that day.

Believers Will Rule the Nations

The saved will be immortal and their bodies will be incorruptible. They will be supernatural and spiritual. In many ways, they will be like Jesus; they are His friends and family. They will take the mandate given to the first Adam to subdue the world, steward it, and manage it. Adam failed, but they will not.

Billions of animals will be there, living in peace, and all of creation will flourish to its optimum potential. Mankind will fully enjoy the pleasures of creativity, invention, work and prosperity. He will be blessed with fun, recreation and glorious fellowship. He will be thrilled with a wealth of friends, and will experience rich fellowship with the Lord. The kingdom of God will have come to earth in answer to the Lord's Prayer. I am sure you remember it; Jesus prayed, **"Thy kingdom come, thy will be done on earth as it is in heaven." Mt. 6:10**

God's kingdom will be on earth, and His people will fully enjoy their reward. Together with the Lord, His people will rule the world with a rod of iron. Non-believers among the nations will live in the glory of God's people. They will be blessed because of the blessing that rests on the saints, and on the land, but some will be unthankful.

Mortals are Blessed as Well

In many ways, immortals and mortals will live a different life during the millennium. One difference will be childbirth and population growth. As the years pass, more and more babies will be born to the mortals, but none to the immortals.

The mortals are the survivors of Armageddon, and many will come into the millennium without making Christ their Lord. The mission to see them become disciples will continue. I can envision many American believers who distinguished themselves before the coming of Christ, being great leaders in the millennium.

In just twenty years, children become adults, marry and begin to have children of their own. In the millennium, they will have grandchildren and great grandchildren and so on, for many generations. Because very few die, billions of unsaved mortals will fill the world. Many of those will become followers of Christ, but a vast multitude will not bow the knee.

Mortals Breed Contempt

As the millennium endures and moves toward its end, a growing disquiet will begin to surface. It will not come from the immortals. They will remember the old life, when they had frail bodies. In the millennium, they will be sons of the Living God, and will not trade that glory for anything. They know the fullness of God's fellowship, and will live like the angels who are there. They could not, and will not turn away from the Lord. They will be totally one with Him for all eternity.

Some mortals in the millennium, however, will take their blessings for granted, and their hearts will fall from gratitude and grace. Most will not have experienced the ravages of sin, or the temptations of the devil. They will have only lived in the millennial kingdom. All they will have known, is the rule of Jesus and His holy ones.

Many of the unsaved will earn positions of authority and responsibility and will begin to influence their community in a direction away from Jerusalem. Some will want to skip out on the feast celebrations. The Lord says that all who refuse to come up to Zion for the Feast of Tabernacles will find that the rains will not fall on their nations and their national productivity will begin to fall. Some will begin to show signs of rebellion (Zechariah 14:17-19). It will soon be time for Satan to appear from the Abyss for his final campaign.

America Once Again

I can only speak, as one who dreams about the future, but I believe that once again, America will shine. Many disciples from God's end-time nation will stand valiantly for the Lord. Disciples from America will reach out with conviction and compassion to teach and persuade the unthankful, the disenchanted and the disgruntled, to follow and obey the Lord.

We are not just told about the great tribulation and the end of the age, the Bible gives us amazing insight into the millennium. It is beyond our reasoning but God gives us glimpses of the rebellion during the millennium.

We read:

"When the thousand years are over, Satan will be released from his prison and will go out to deceive the nations in the four corners of the earth – Gog and Magog – to gather them for battle. In number they are like the sand on the seashore. They marched across the breadth of the earth and surrounded the camp of God's people, the city he loves. But fire came down from heaven and devoured them. And the devil, who deceived them, was thrown into the lake of burning sulfur, where the beast and the false prophet had been thrown." Rev. 20:7-10

Those who gather to fight the Lord are called Gog and Magog. Satan will be released from his prison and will go out to deceive the nations in the four corners of the earth – to gather them for battle. In number they are like the sand on the seashore.

Israel Surrounded Again

Fear will fill some of the hearts of the mortals who live in Israel. Gog and Magog will surround the city of Jerusalem.

God allows the rebels' military maneuvers to go that far, but no further. They will not have time to strike. Not one person will be killed before God intervenes. The uprising will be permitted for one reason, to reveal the hearts of men, to let the world and the universe see who has chosen to be God's enemy.

Fire From Heaven

When all of Magog has gathered for battle, God Almighty will make a preemptive strike. No enemy weapon will fire before the heavens open. Suddenly, and without warning, fire will fall on the enemies of God. Jesus will be on his throne in Jerusalem, but the Almighty will fight this battle from heaven. No angel will appear, no human will lift a militant hand; it will be God himself who will destroy the approaching army. **"But fire came down from heaven and devoured them." Rev. 20:9**

Satan's Destiny

The devil, who deceived the nations, will be cast into the Lake of Fire where the beast and the false prophet were thrown one thousand years earlier. It is a lake of burning sulfur. There, fallen angels will suffer and that is Satan's destiny. He cannot avoid it, or delay it. His eternal doom is sealed already and all of his schemes for chaos and destruction, will not affect the final outcome.

Satan cannot take a human soul with him to Hell by wishing for it. Each person will stand or fall before God alone. The devil has hindered and hurt many during their lifetime, but he has no eternal claims on the souls of men. He does not rule in Hell, he is just a prisoner.

Face to Face with God

"No longer will there be any curse. The throne of God and of the Lamb will be in the city, and his servants will serve him. They will see his face." Rev. 22:3-4

Eternity has still more blessings. For the first time since the Garden of Eden, the Bible says that man will be able to see God face to face. Throughout history, no man could see God's face and live. It is amazing; in eternity we will see His face (Rev. 22:4). This happens only after the curse is fully gone. Finally, all barriers between God and man will be removed and both the Almighty and the Lamb, will dwell in the newly formed city of Jerusalem.

During the great millennium only Christ's throne appears on earth, but at the end of the millennium, after the Father's final judgments, God Almighty will also live and rule on earth. The throne of God moves from heaven to earth, and our fellowship with Him is made complete.

The Great Presentation

Then, Christ will give the kingdom back to His Father. This is the climax of eternity, as we know it. Ages before, God gave His Son the kingdoms of the earth, including America. Christ accomplished His task. Everything has now been brought under His feet. When everything will be made perfect, it will be time to give the kingdom back to God the Father. Along with all of the other nations, Jesus will present America unto the Father.

"Then the end will come, when he hands over the kingdom to God the Father after he has destroyed all dominion, authority and power. For he must reign until he has put all his enemies under his feet." 1 Cor. 15:24-25

Light of the World

Jesus has always been the Light of the World and the Light of Men (see John 1:4-5). That means that the right direction for man and the total provision for man's life are found in Him. All who try to make their own light or follow a different light, find a false light. They find darkness, and no light at all.

In eternity, God will give us new light. He and the Lamb are our light. All knowledge, wisdom, instruction and direction come from Him. Forever, He is the light of man, the light of the world and the light that extends to the far reaches of the universe.

All who live, will live in that glorious light. That means that no one will be inferior, or be in lack. Each person will fly to the height of his personal destiny.

For Americans, we thank God for our nation, and for this amazing home base, but it is just a launching pad. We will serve and reign with Him. We will conquer new horizons and bring distant territories under His domain. We will receive authority from God and rule with Him beyond the stars.

Notes

[i] "Emma Lazarus." Wikipedia: The Free Encyclopedia. Wikimedia Foundation, Inc. 22nd July 2004. Web. 22 Apr. 2015

[ii] Rabbi Shraga Simmons. Naming a Baby. June 15, 2002. The Jewish Website. Viewed April 8, 2015. http://www.aish.com/jl/48961326.html

[iii] Rabbi Shraga Simmons. Naming a Baby. June 15, 2002. The Jewish Website. Viewed April 8, 2015. http://www.aish.com/jl/48961326.html

[iv] "Religion and the Founding of the American Republic". American as a Religious Refuge:. The Seventeenth Century, Part 1, Eliot's Algonquin Language Bible. Library of Congress. Accessed May 5, 2015 <http//www.loc.gov/exhibits/religion/re101.html>

[v] "Religion and the Founding of the American Republic". American as a Religious Refuge:. The Seventeenth Century. Library of Congress. Accessed May 5, 2015. <http://www.loc.gov/exhibits/religion/rel01.html>

[vi] "Religion and the Founding of the American Republic". American as a Religious Refuge:. The Seventeenth Century. Library of Congress. Accessed May 5, 2015. <http://www.loc.gov/exhibits/religion/rel01.html>

[vii] "Religion and the Founding of the American Republic". American as a Religious Refuge:. The Seventeenth Century. Library of Congress. Accessed May 5, 2015. <http://www.loc.gov/exhibits/religion/rel01.html#obj001>

[viii] "Religion and the Founding of the American Republic". American as a Religious Refuge:. The Seventeenth Century. Library of Congress. Accessed May 5, 2015. <http://www.loc.gov/exhibits/religion/rel01.html#obj009>

[ix] "Religion and the Founding of the American Republic". American as a Religious Refuge:. The Seventeenth Century. Library of Congress. Accessed May 5, 2015. <http://www.loc.gov/exhibits/religion/rel01.html#obj005>

[x] "Religion and the Founding of the American Republic". American as a Religious Refuge:. The Seventeenth Century. Library of Congress. Accessed May 5, 2015. <http://www.loc.gov/exhibits/religion/rel01.html#obj004>

Notes continued

[xi] "Religion and the Founding of the American Republic". American as a Religious Refuge:. The Seventeenth Century. Library of Congress. Accessed May 5, 2015. <http://www.loc.gov/exhibits/religion/rel01.html#obj003>

[xii] "The Diary of William Bradford". The Founding Faith Archive. From April 2, 2015 <http://www.beliefnet.com/resourcelib/docs/149/Diary_of_William_Bradford>

[xiii] Lindsay Koshgariam, "Penny on the Dollar" National Priorities Project. Aug 4, 2104. Accessed May 3, 2015. <https://www.nationalpriorities.org/blog/2014/08/12/penny-dollar-us-foreign-aid-about-one-percent-spending>

[xiv] "Key Figures 2013" A Development Initiative. Accessed May 4, 2015. <http://www.global humanitarian assistance.org/countryprofile/united-states>

[xv] "General Analysis on US Military Expansion and Intervention" Global Policy Forum. Accessed May 5, 2015. <https://www.globalpolicy.org/us-military-expansion-and-intervention/general-analysis-on-us-military-expansion-and-intervention.html>

[xvi] "Office of U.S. Foreign Disaster Assistance" Updated July 23, 2014. US Aid. Accessed June 15, 2015. <https://www.usaid.gov>

[xvii] "Statistics" About Missions. Accessed June 15, 2015. <http://www.aboutmissions.org/statistics.html>

[xviii] "Missions Statistics" Message Ministries & Missions. Accessed May 8, 2015. <http://www.messagemissions.com/mission-statistics> page 3

[xix] "Missions Statistics" Message Ministries & Missions. Accessed May 8, 2015. <http://www.messagemissions.com/mission-statistics> page 4

[xx] "Missions Statistics" Message Ministries & Missions. Accessed May 8, 2015. <http://www.messagemissions.com/mission-statistics> page 6

[xxi] Melisssa Steffan. "The Surprising Countries Most Missionaries Are Sent From and Go To". July 25, 2013. Gleanings. Accessed April 2, 2015. <http://www.christianitytoday.com/gleanings/2013/july/missionaries-countries-sent-received-csgc-gordon-conwell.html>

Notes continued

[xxii] "Missions Statistics" Message Ministries & Missions. Accessed May 8, 2015. <http://www.messagemissions.com/mission-statistics> page 5

[xxiii] Donald Moran. "Haym Salomon – The Revolutionary's Indispensable Financial Genius". A Revolutionary War Historical Article. Accessed May 6, 2015. <http://www.revolutionarywararchives.org/salomon.html>

[xxiv] John McTernan. As America Has Done To Israel. (New Kensington, PA: Whitaker House, 2008) 78.

[xxv] Rabbi Micah Peltz. "George Washington Changed the Way Jews Live in the U.S." Feb 22, 2012. Haaretz. Accessed June 15, 2015. <http://www.haaretz.com/jewish-world/george-washington-changed-the-way-jews-live-in-the-u-s-1.414118>

[xxvi] "US Presidents & Israel: Quotes About Jewish Homeland & Israel". American-Israeli Cooperative Enterprise. Accessed June 15 2015. <https://www.jewishvirtuallibrary.org/jsource/US-Israel/presquote.html>

[xxvii] The NIV Study Bible, 10th Anniversary Edition, Zondervan Publishing House, Grand Rapids, MI 49530, USA, Study Notes, pg. 1372

[xxviii] "Tarshish" Bible History Online. Easton's Bible Dictionary. Accessed June 16, 2015. <http://www.bible-history.com/eastons/T/Tarshish>

[xxix] Gary Langer. "Poll: Most Americans Say They're Christian". July 18, 2105. ABC News. Accessed July 22, 2015. <http://abcnews.go.com/US/story?id=90356>

[xxx] Niall Kilkenny. "The Defeat of the "Invincible" Armada". 2007. Accessed Aug 6, 2015. <http://www.reformation.org/spanish-armada.html>

[xxxi] Remarks to Baltimore Presbyterian Synod on October 24, 1863 (CWAL VI:536)

[xxxii] Matthew White. "Necrometrcis". Updated September 2010. Accessed July 16, 2015. <http://necrometrics.com/all20c.htm>

Notes continued

xxxiii John McTernan. <u>As America Has Done To Israel</u>. (New Kensington, PA: Whitaker House, 2008), 218.

xxxiv Iain H. Murray, <u>The Puritan Hope; Revival and Interpretation of Prophecy,</u> (Edinburgh, UK: Banner of Truth, 1971) 61.

xxxv Iain H. Murray, <u>The Puritan Hope; Revival and Interpretation of Prophecy,</u> (Edinburgh, UK: Banner of Truth, 1971) 113.

xxxvi Iain H. Murray, <u>The Puritan Hope; Revival and Interpretation of Prophecy,</u> (Edinburgh, UK: Banner of Truth, 1971) 256.

xxxvii "Christianity In China" Updated 2014. BillionBibles.org. Accessed June 23, 2015. <http://www.billionbibles.org/china/how-many-christians-in-china.html>

xxxviii Tony Cauchi, "The History of Revivals of Religion – William E. Allen" Updated 2015. The Revival Library. Accessed July 20, 2015. <http://www.revival-library.org/index.php/catalogues-menu/general-histories/history-of-revivals-of-religion>

www.ingramcontent.com/pod-product-compliance
Lightning Source LLC
Chambersburg PA
CBHW070534010526
44118CB00012B/1127